HERE BEGINS THE GOSPEL

HERE BEGINS THE GOSPEL

A READING BOOK

SELECTIONS FROM
THE NEW ENGLISH BIBLE

COMPILED BY
BETTY E. STONE

UNITED CHURCH PRESS
BOSTON · PHILADELPHIA

Grateful acknowledgment is made to the following artists, photographers, photographic services, and museums for the use of the material on the following pages: Anderson, Rome, p. 74; The Bettmann Archive, pp. 44 and 53; Boston Book and Art Shop, pp. 1 and 7; Mr. and Mrs. Ross W. Sloniker Collection of Twentieth Century Biblical and Religious Prints, The Cincinnati Art Museum, p. 62; Jerome Halberstadt, p. 42; Arthur Polonsky, 17; Peter C. Schlaifer, pp. 32 and 60; Kenneth Thompson, pp. 5 and 51; Art Wood, pp. 34 and 82.

The scripture quotations in this publication are from *The New English Bible, New Testament* © The Delegates of the Oxford University Press and The Syndics of the Cambridge University Press 1961. Reprinted by permission.

This book is part of the United Church Curriculum, prepared and published by the Division of Christian Education and the Division of Publication of the United Church Board for Homeland Ministries.

TABLE OF CONTENTS

ABOUT

HAVE YOU EVER COME HOME and found all the furniture in the living room rearranged? Things look different. You notice a chair that you never noticed before. There is a picture on the wall that you're sure you never saw before. Was it there all the time? The whole room looks so different.

Often, when we read a different translation of the Bible we find that the same thing happens. We notice things we never noticed before. We catch a new picture of things. New truths leap out. The whole story seems different.

That is why this book has been compiled from a recent translation of the New Testament—*The New English Bible.* It is to help you think afresh about some of the stories, teachings, and words that you have heard many times. Things are rearranged, different.

The writers of the New Testament were not eager to present a chronological account of the life of Jesus. They were not writing biography. The history, geography, sociology, and economics of the time of Jesus did not concern them very much. They didn't have time for that. They were too busy bearing witness to an experience with an amazing person, Jesus of Nazareth, who was for them Jesus Christ, the Son of God. The Gospels they wrote, the sermons they preached, and the letters they sent were primarily to convince others that Jesus was the Christ. They wrote and preached to encourage other Christians who were being persecuted. They wrote to help struggling churches to be faithful to their Lord. They had surprising good news, a gospel, to share with everyone. That is why the first four books of the New Testament are called "gospels." They are "good news" for all people.

This book contains an account of the life and teachings and ministry of Jesus. It is based primarily on the gospel account

THIS BOOK

"according to Mark." However, you will find some passages from Matthew, Luke, John, and Acts, in order to make the witness more complete. The writer of the Gospel of John wrote: "There were indeed many other signs that Jesus performed in the presence of his disciples, which are not recorded in this book. Those here written have been recorded in order that you may hold the faith that Jesus is the Christ, the Son of God, and that through this faith you may possess eternal life by his name" (John 20: 30–31). This book, too, is written that you may hold the faith that Jesus is the Christ, the Son of God.

The life, teachings, and ministry of Jesus invite each of us to participate in a journey,

a pilgrimage,
a search.

To help you in your journey you will find brief introductions to each section of scripture that will help set the stage (arrange the room, so to speak) for the story. As you walk into the room try to imagine what it must have felt like to be there almost two thousand years ago. What was the country like? How were the people feeling? How did they respond to what they heard and saw?

Then, think about what these things mean for us today. What do they say to a young person like you? To help you in your pilgrimage you will find at the end of each chapter the response of a modern young person as he reacts to the events in the life of Christ.

Perhaps his questions will help you form your own questions.
Perhaps his doubts will help you meet your own doubts.
Perhaps his response will help you to make your response!

"Here begins the Gospel of Jesus Christ the Son of God."

—Mark 1:1

I THE COMING OF CHRIST

Rembrandt   THE BAPTISM OF CHRIST

THE TIME: The fifteenth year of the reign of Tiberius, emperor of Rome.

THE PLACE: Galilee, a Roman province in Judea governed by Herod Antipas.

THE EVENT: A journey from Nazareth to the river Jordan.

You would hardly expect anyone to have taken particular notice when a little group of people from Galilee set out on a journey to the Jordan River. Many people had made the trip. They had come from all over Judea, even from as far as Jerusalem, to hear the strange new prophet, John. And no wonder . . . John was different.

 He wore strange clothing,
  and spent long weeks in the desert, alone.

But even stranger than the way he looked were the things he said:
 "Repent; . . .
  The kingdom of Heaven is upon you! . . .
  'Prepare a way for the Lord.'"

The people who heard him began to wonder. Could it be that at last, after so many years of cruel oppression and poverty and injustice, the Hebrew people would again be free? Would a new Jewish king come to power? Or would the Lord God himself come to rule his people?

Expectation ran high. There was much conversation in the market place, in the synagogues, and in the temple at Jerusalem. The Roman rulers began to be suspicious.

John proclaimed:
 Repent . . . be baptized.
 Begin a new life.
 Be ready for the kingdom.

And many came and confessed their sins, and were baptized. Among them was Jesus of Nazareth, unnoticed and unknown.

And here begins the story . . .

PREPARING THE WAY

Here begins the Gospel of Jesus Christ the Son of God.

In the prophet Isaiah it stands written: 'Here is my herald whom I send on ahead of you, and he will prepare your way. A voice crying aloud in the wilderness, "Prepare a way for the Lord; clear a straight path for him."' And so it was that John the Baptist appeared in the wilderness proclaiming a baptism in token of repentance, for the forgiveness of sins; and they flocked to him from the whole Judaean country-side and the city of Jerusalem, and were baptized by him in the River Jordan, confessing their sins.

John was dressed in a rough coat of camel's hair, with a leather belt round his waist, and he fed on locusts and wild honey. His proclamation ran: 'After me comes one who is mightier than I. I am not fit to unfasten his shoes. I have baptized you with water; he will baptize you with the Holy Spirit.'

It happened at this time that Jesus came from Nazareth in Galilee and was baptized in the Jordan by John. At the moment when he came up out of the water, he saw the heavens torn open and the Spirit, like a dove, descending upon him. And a voice spoke from heaven: 'Thou art my Son, my Beloved; on thee my favour rests.'

Thereupon the Spirit sent him away into the wilderness, and there he remained for forty days tempted by Satan.

—Mark 1:1–13a

MEETING TEMPTATION

Full of the Holy Spirit, Jesus returned from the Jordan, and for forty days was led by the Spirit up and down the wilderness and tempted by the devil.

All that time he had nothing to eat, and at the end of it he was famished. The devil said to him, 'If you are the Son of God, tell this stone to become bread.' Jesus answered, 'Scripture says, "Man cannot live on bread alone." '

Next the devil led him up and showed him in a flash all the kingdoms of the world. 'All this dominion will I give to you,' he said, 'and the glory that goes with it; for it has been put in my hands and I can give it to anyone I choose. You have only to do homage to me and it shall all be yours.' Jesus answered him, 'Scripture says, "You shall do homage to the Lord your God and worship him alone." '

The devil took him to Jerusalem and set him on the parapet of the temple. 'If you are the Son of God,' he said, 'throw yourself down; for Scripture says, "He will give his angels orders to take care of you", and again, "They will support you in their arms for fear you should strike your foot against a stone." ' Jesus answered him, 'It has been said, "You are not to test the Lord your God." '

So, having come to the end of all his temptations, the devil departed, biding his time.   *—Luke 4:1–13*

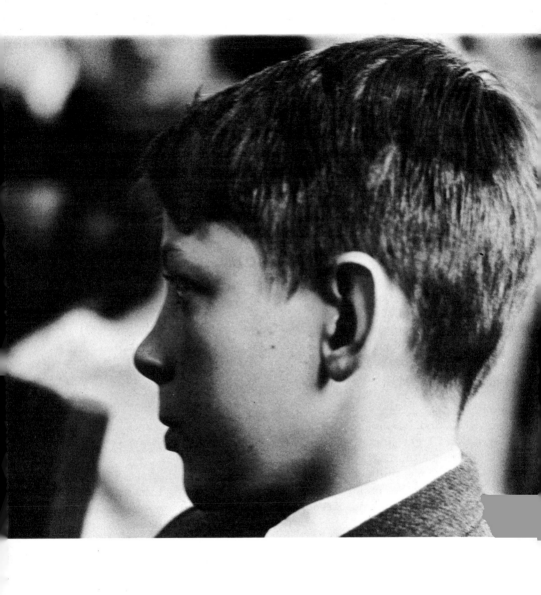

Sometimes you don't even know it,
When something important is happening to a person.
Maybe you're hurt, or angry inside,
    And no one even knows.
Or perhaps you're tempted to do something wrong,
    And no one knows how hard it was to decide.
And sometimes you discover some tremendous thing about yourself,
    And nobody has any idea what's happened.
    Maybe you don't understand it all yourself.

I wonder if that's what happened to him, to Jesus.
Perhaps that's why he went off alone to think about it all.
Imagine having God speak to you!

It's kind of good to get away and think things out—
    To get away from school and clubs,
    From parents and TV and things,
And try to figure out
    who you really are,
    why you were born,
    what you're going to be.
And make some decisions about life.

O God, help me to understand myself, why I act the way I do. Sometimes I get so mad at myself. I guess you must get pretty disgusted with me too.

Help me, too, to care about other people, how they feel inside. Help me to see that important things may be happening to them, because of what is done or said. Keep me from hurting others by things I say and do. Amen.

II IN GALILEE:
SUCCESS AND OPPOSITION

Rembrandt   THE HEALING OF A BLIND MAN

Jesus stood up in his own synagogue, before his own family and friends, and began to speak. It wasn't easy. Many knew him—from his childhood up. They knew him as a carpenter in Nazareth.

But something had happened to him on that trip to the Jordan River. Something had happened to him during the days he spent alone in the wilderness.

He began to teach,
    and to preach,
        and to heal.
What had happened to him?

The people were amazed. They said:
    —"Where does he get it from? How does he work such miracles?"
    —"What is this? He speaks with authority!"
    —"Never before have we seen the like!"

Crowds began to come—
    to listen to him,
        and to be healed.

There were in Galilee some scribes and Pharisees who were very particular about the religious laws of the Hebrew people. They spent their days studying and interpreting to the people the hundreds of laws and rules of the Scriptures—about what to eat, whom to associate with, what to do and not to do on the Sabbath. When Jesus began to heal people and to forgive sins, when he ate with tax collectors and sinners, when he and his disciples picked grain on the Sabbath, the Pharisees were angry. He was breaking religious tradition!

The scribes and Pharisees said:
    —"Why does this fellow talk like this?
    This is blasphemy!
    Who but God alone can forgive sins?"
    —"He eats with tax-gatherers and sinners!"
    —"Look, why are they doing what is forbidden on the Sabbath?"

But despite success and opposition, Jesus continued to teach and to heal. And he called twelve disciples to help him proclaim the gospel.

JESUS BEGAN PREACHING

After John had been arrested, Jesus came into Galilee proclaiming the Gospel of God: 'The time has come; the kingdom of God is upon you; repent, and believe the Gospel.'

—Mark 1:14–15

And reports about him spread through the whole countryside. He taught in their synagogues and all men sang his praises.

So he came to Nazareth, where he had been brought up, and went to the synagogue on the Sabbath day as he regularly did. He stood up to read the lesson and was handed the scroll of the prophet Isaiah. He opened the scroll and found the passage which says,

'The spirit of the Lord is upon me because he has anointed me;
He has sent me to announce good news to the poor,
To proclaim release for prisoners and recovery of sight for the blind;
To let the broken victims go free,
To proclaim the year of the Lord's favour.'

He rolled up the scroll, gave it back to the attendant, and sat down; and all eyes in the synagogue were fixed on him.

He began to speak: 'Today', he said, 'in your very hearing this text has come true.' There was a general stir of admiration; they were surprised that words of such grace should fall from his lips.

—Luke 4:14b–22a

And the large congregation who heard him were amazed and said, 'Where does he get it from?', and, 'What wisdom is this that has been given him?', and, 'How does he work such miracles? Is not this the carpenter, the son of Mary, the brother of James and Joseph and Judas and Simon? And are not his sisters here with us?' So they fell foul of him. Jesus said to them, 'A prophet

9

will always be held in honour except in his home town, and among his kinsmen and family.' He could work no miracle there, except that he put his hands on a few sick people and healed them; and he was taken aback by their want of faith.

—Mark 6: 2b–6

HE CALLED DISCIPLES

Jesus was walking by the shore of the Sea of Galilee when he saw Simon and his brother Andrew on the lake at work with a casting-net; for they were fishermen. Jesus said to them, 'Come with me, and I will make you fishers of men.' And at once they left their nets and followed him.

When he had gone a little further he saw James son of Zebedee and his brother John, who were in the boat overhauling their nets. He called them; and, leaving their father Zebedee in the boat with the hired men, they went off to follow him.

They came to Capernaum, and on the Sabbath he went to synagogue and began to teach. The people were astounded at his teaching, for, unlike the doctors of the law, he taught with a note of authority. Now there was a man in the synagogue possessed by an unclean spirit. He shrieked: 'What do you want with us, Jesus of Nazareth? Have you come to destroy us? I know who you are—the Holy One of God.' Jesus rebuked him: 'Be silent', he said, 'and come out of him.' And the unclean spirit threw the man into convulsions and with a loud cry left him. They were all dumbfounded and began to ask one another, 'What is this? A new kind of teaching! He speaks with authority. When he gives orders, even the unclean spirits submit.' The news spread rapidly, and he was soon spoken of all over the district of Galilee. *—Mark 1: 16–28*

CONFLICT ABOUT HEALING

Very early next morning he got up and went out. He went away to a lonely spot and remained there in prayer. But Simon and his companions searched him out, found him, and said, 'They are all looking for you.' He answered, 'Let us move on to the country towns in the neighbourhood; I have to proclaim my message there also; that is what I came out to do.' So all through Galilee he went, preaching in the synagogues and casting out the devils.

Once he was approached by a leper, who knelt before him begging his help. 'If only you will,' said the man, 'you can cleanse me.' In warm indignation Jesus stretched out his hand, touched him, and said, 'Indeed I will; be clean again.' The leprosy left him immediately, and he was clean. Then he dismissed him with this stern warning: 'Be sure you say nothing to anybody. Go and show yourself to the priest, and make the offering laid down by Moses for your cleansing; that will certify the cure.' But the man went out and made the whole story public; he spread it far and wide, until Jesus could no longer show himself in any town, but stayed outside in the open country. Even so, people kept coming to him from all quarters.

When after some days he returned to Capernaum, the news went round that he was at home; and such a crowd collected that the space in front of the door was not big enough to hold them. And while he was proclaiming the message to them, a man was brought who was paralysed. Four men were carrying him, but because of the crowd they could not get him near. So they opened up the roof over the place where Jesus was, and when they had broken throught they lowered the stretcher on which the paralysed man was lying. When Jesus saw their faith, he said to the paralysed man, 'My son, your sins are forgiven.'

Now there were some lawyers sitting there and they thought to themselves, 'Why does the fellow talk like that? This is blasphemy! Who but God alone can forgive sins?' Jesus knew in his own mind that this was what they were thinking, and said to them: 'Why do you harbour thoughts like these? Is it easier to say to this paralysed man, "Your sins are forgiven", or to say,

"Stand up, take your bed, and walk"? But to convince you that the Son of Man has the right on earth to forgive sins'—he turned to the paralysed man—'I say to you, stand up, take your bed, and go home.' And he got up, took his stretcher at once, and went out in full view of them all, so that they were astounded and praised God. 'Never before', they said, 'have we seen the like.'

—Mark 1:35—2:12

CALLING MATTHEW

Once more he went away to the lake-side. All the crowd came to him, and he taught them there. As he went along, he saw Levi son of Alphaeus at his seat in the custom-house, and said to him, 'Follow me'; and Levi rose and followed him.

—Mark 2:13–14

CONFLICT ABOUT EATING WITH SINNERS

When Jesus was at table in his house, many bad characters— tax-gatherers and others—were seated with him and his disciples; for there were many who followed him. Some doctors of the law who were Pharisees noticed him eating in this bad company, and said to his disciples, 'He eats with tax-gatherers and sinners!' Jesus overheard and said to them, 'It is not the healthy that need a doctor, but the sick; I did not come to invite virtuous people, but sinners.' *—Mark 2:15–17*

CONFLICT ABOUT FORGIVING SINS

One of the Pharisees invited him to dinner; he went to the Pharisee's house and took his place at table. A woman who was living an immoral life in the town had learned that Jesus was dining in the Pharisee's house and had brought oil of myrrh in a small flask. She took her place behind him, by his feet, weeping. His feet were wetted with her tears and she wiped them with her hair, kissing them and anointing them with the myrrh. When his

host the Pharisee saw this he said to himself, 'If this fellow were a real prophet, he would know who this woman is that touches him, and what sort of woman she is, a sinner.' Jesus took him up and said, 'Simon, I have something to say to you.' 'Speak on, Master', said he. 'Two men were in debt to a money-lender: one owed him five hundred silver pieces, the other fifty. As neither had anything to pay with he let them both off. Now, which will love him most?' Simon replied, 'I should think the one that was let off most.' 'You are right', said Jesus. Then turning to the woman, he said to Simon, 'You see this woman? I came to your house: you provided no water for my feet; but this woman has made my feet wet with her tears and wiped them with her hair. You gave me no kiss; but she has been kissing my feet ever since I came in. You did not anoint my head with oil; but she has anointed my feet with myrrh. And so, I tell you, her great love proves that her many sins have been forgiven; where little has been forgiven, little love is shown.' Then he said to her, 'Your sins are forgiven.' The other guests began to ask themselves, 'Who is this, that he can forgive sins?' But he said to the woman, 'Your faith has saved you; go in peace.'
—*Luke 7:36–50*

CONFLICT ABOUT THE SABBATH

One Sabbath he was going through the cornfields; and his disciples, as they went, began to pluck ears of corn. The Pharisees said to him, 'Look, why are they doing what is forbidden on the Sabbath?' He answered, 'Have you never read what David did when he and his men were hungry and had nothing to eat? He went into the House of God, in the time of Abiathar the High Priest, and ate the consecrated loaves, though no one but a priest is allowed to eat them, and even gave them to his men.'

He also said to them, 'The Sabbath was made for the sake of man and not man for the Sabbath: therefore the Son of Man is sovereign even over the Sabbath.'

On another occasion when he went to synagogue, there was a man in the congregation who had a withered arm; and they were watching to see whether Jesus would cure him on the Sabbath, so that they could bring a charge against him. He said to the man with the withered arm, 'Come and stand out here.' Then he turned to them: 'Is it permitted to do good or to do evil on the Sabbath, to save life or to kill?' They had nothing to say; and, looking round at them with anger and sorrow at their obstinate stupidity, he said to the man, 'Stretch out your arm.' He stretched it out and his arm was restored. But the Pharisees, on leaving the synagogue, began plotting against him with the partisans of Herod to see how they could make away with him.

—Mark 2:23–3:6

APPOINTING DISCIPLES

He then went up into the hill-country and called the men he wanted; and they went and joined him. He appointed twelve as his companions, whom he would send out to proclaim the Gospel, with a commission to drive out devils. So he appointed the Twelve: to Simon he gave the name Peter; then came the sons of Zebedee, James and his brother John, to whom he gave the name Boanerges, Sons of Thunder; then Andrew and Philip and Bartholomew and Matthew and Thomas and James the son of Alphaeus and Thaddaeus and Simon, a member of the Zealot party, and Judas Iscariot, the man who betrayed him. *—Mark 3:13–19*

FOLLOW ME

As they were going along the road a man said to him, 'I will follow you wherever you go.' Jesus answered, 'Foxes have their holes, the birds their roosts; but the Son of Man has nowhere to lay his head.' To another he said, 'Follow me', but the man replied, 'Let me go and bury my father first.' Jesus said, 'Leave the dead to bury their dead; you must go and announce the kingdom of God.'

Yet another said, 'I will follow you, sir; but let me first say good-bye to my people at home.' To him Jesus said, 'No one who sets his hand to the plough and then keeps looking back is fit for the kingdom of God.'   —*Luke 9:57–62*

Then his mother and his brothers arrived, and remaining ouside sent in a message asking him to come out to them. A crowd was sitting round and word was brought to him: 'Your mother and your brothers are outside asking for you.' He replied, 'Who is my mother? Who are my brothers?' And looking round at those who were sitting in the circle about him he said, 'Here are my mother and my brothers. Whoever does the will of God is my brother, my sister, my mother.'   —*Mark 3:31–35*

SENT ON A MISSION

On one of his teaching journeys round the villages he summoned the Twelve and sent them out in pairs on a mission. He gave them authority over unclean spirits, and instructed them to take nothing for the journey beyond a stick: no bread, no pack, no money in their belts. They might wear sandals, but not a second coat. 'When you are admitted to a house', he added, 'stay there until you leave those parts. At any place where they will not receive you or listen to you, shake the dust off your feet as you leave, as a warning to them.' So they set out and called publicly for repentance. They drove out many devils, and many sick people they anointed with oil and cured.   —*Mark 6:7–13*

It must have been awfully hard for Jesus
To stand up and speak like that,
In front of his friends and family,
Especially about some strange new kingdom.
I admire him for that.
But what an odd thing to talk about.
What a strange kingdom!

15

Repentance is the condition for membership?
"Believe" is the oath of allegiance?
The promises:
    good news for the poor,
    release for prisoners,
    sight for the blind.

What is that to me?
I believe what I want to,
Why should I repent?
I'm not poor,
    I'm not imprisoned,
        I'm not blind!
I'm young, and full of life, and free!

And by the way, who made you king?
You, Jesus, a carpenter's son.
What right had you
    to upset the traditions of the law?
By what authority
    did you heal the sick?
Who gave you the power
    to forgive?
By what authority
    did you draw men to discipleship?
Who gave you the right
    to make bold claims?

But even as my questions mount,
I'm strangely drawn—
What power did you have, young carpenter,
To call strong fishermen away from nets,
To draw the tax-collector from his work?
What power have you, carpenter,
That I'm compelled to follow too!

God, I need your help. I've tried, but so much of this is hard to understand. So much of it seems unimportant in my world of space shots and baseball games. Deep inside I doubt, I challenge. Sometimes I just don't care. Help me. Amen.

III TEACHINGS

Arthur Polinsky   JESUS TEACHING

Wherever he was—
    on a hillside,
    in a home,
    in a market-place,
    along a road,
    or by a lake—

Jesus took time to be with people,
    to listen to them,
    to teach them about the Father,
    and of love for one another.

He talked
    to two, or twelve, or hundreds,
    to a lawyer, or to a child;
    wherever men looked up in need
    and questioned him:

        —What is the kingdom, anyway?
        —What is the gospel, the good news?
        —What is the law, the way, the truth?
        —What is the will of the Father?
        —What should I believe?
        —What is eternal life?
        —Teach us how to pray.

Filled with compassion for the crowd,
And afire with the truth of the living God,
He taught them with authority.

THE CROWDS CAME

Jesus went away to the lake-side with his disciples. Great numbers from Galilee, Judaea and Jerusalem, Idumaea and Trans-jordan, and the neighbourhood of Tyre and Sidon, heard what he was doing and came to see him.   —*Mark 3:7–8*

HE TAUGHT THEM:
ABOUT BEING BLEST

When he saw the crowds he went up the hill. There he took his seat, and when his disciples had gathered round him he began to address them. And this is the teaching he gave:

'How blest are those who know that they are poor;
　　the kingdom of Heaven is theirs.
How blest are the sorrowful;
　　they shall find consolation.
How blest are those of a gentle spirit;
　　they shall have the earth for their possession.
How blest are those who hunger and thirst to see right prevail;
　　they shall be satisfied.
How blest are those who show mercy;
　　mercy shall be shown to them.
How blest are those whose hearts are pure;
　　they shall see God.
How blest are the peacemakers;
　　God shall call them his sons.
How blest are those who have suffered persecution
　　　for the cause of right;
　　the kingdom of Heaven is theirs.

How blest you are, when you suffer insults and persecution and every kind of calumny for my sake. Accept it with gladness and exultation, for you have a rich reward in heaven; in the same way they persecuted the prophets before you.'   —*Matthew 5:1–12*

ABOUT BEING WITNESSES

'You are salt to the world. And if salt becomes tasteless, how is its saltness to be restored? It is now good for nothing but to be thrown away and trodden underfoot.

'You are light for all the world. A town that stands on a hill cannot be hidden. When a lamp is lit, it is not put under the meal-tub, but on the lamp-stand, where it gives light to everyone in the house. And you, like the lamp, must shed light among your fellows, so that, when they see the good you do, they may give praise to your Father in heaven.' —*Matthew 5:13–16*

ABOUT HATE AND LOVE

'You have learned that our forefathers were told, "Do not commit murder; anyone who commits murder must be brought to judgement." But what I tell you is this: Anyone who nurses anger against his brother must be brought to judgement. If he abuses his brother he must answer for it to the court; if he sneers at him he will have to answer for it in the fires of hell.

'If, when you are bringing your gift to the altar, you suddenly remember that your brother has a grievance against you, leave your gift where it is before the altar. First go and make your peace with your brother, and only then come back and offer your gift.'
—*Matthew 5:21–24*

'You have learned that they were told, "An eye for an eye, and a tooth for a tooth." But what I tell you is this: Do not set yourself against the man who wrongs you. If someone slaps you on the right cheek, turn and offer him your left. If a man wants to sue you for your shirt, let him have your coat as well. If a man in authority makes you go one mile, go with him two. Give when you are asked to give; and do not turn your back on a man who wants to borrow.

'You have learned that they were told, "Love your neighbour, hate your enemy." But what I tell you is this: Love your enemies

20

and pray for your persecutors; only so can you be children of your heavenly Father, who makes his sun rise on good and bad alike, and sends the rain on the honest and the dishonest. If you love only those who love you, what reward can you expect? Surely the tax-gatherers do as much as that. And if you greet only your brothers, what is there extraordinary about that? Even the heathen do as much. You must therefore be all goodness, just as your heavenly Father is all good.'   —*Matthew 5:38–48*

ABOUT INNER MOTIVES AND WORSHIP

'Be careful not to make a show of your religion before men; if you do, no reward awaits you in your Father's house in heaven.

'Thus, when you do some act of charity, do not announce it with a flourish of trumpets, as the hypocrites do in synagogue and in the streets to win admiration from men. I tell you this: they have their reward already. No; when you do some act of charity, do not let your left hand know what your right is doing; your good deed must be secret, and your Father who sees what is done in secret will reward you.

'In your prayers do not go babbling on like the heathen, who imagine that the more they say the more likely they are to be heard. Do not imitate them. Your Father knows what your needs are before you ask him.

'This is how you should pray:
"Our Father in heaven,
Thy name be hallowed;
Thy kingdom come,
Thy will be done,
On earth as in heaven.
Give us today our daily bread.
Forgive us the wrong we have done,
As we have forgiven those who have wronged us.
And do not bring us to the test,
But save us from the evil one." '   —*Matthew 6:1–4, 7–13*

ABOUT JUDGING

'Pass no judgement, and you will not be judged. For as you judge others, so you will yourselves be judged, and whatever measure you deal out to others will be dealt back to you. Why do you look at the speck of sawdust in your brother's eye, with never a thought for the great plank in your own? Or how can you say to your brother, "Let me take the speck out of your eye", when all the time there is that plank in your own? You hypocrite! First take the plank out of your own eye, and then you will see clearly to take the speck out of your brother's.' —*Matthew 7:1–5*

ABOUT TRUSTING IN GOD

'Ask, and you will receive; seek, and you will find; knock, and the door will be opened. For everyone who asks receives, he who seeks finds, and to him who knocks, the door will be opened.

'Is there a man among you who will offer his son a stone when he asks for bread, or a snake when he asks for fish? If you, then, bad as you are, know how to give your children what is good for them, how much more will your heavenly Father give good things to those who ask him!

'Always treat others as you would like them to treat you: that is the Law and the prophets.' —*Matthew 7:7–12*

ABOUT HEARING AND DOING

'What then of the man who hears these words of mine and acts upon them? He is like a man who had the sense to build his house on rock. The rain came down, the floods rose, the wind blew, and beat upon that house; but it did not fall, because its foundations were on rock. But what of the man who hears these words of mine and does not act upon them? He is like a man who was foolish enough to build his house on sand. The rain came down, the floods rose, the wind blew, and beat upon that house; down it fell with a great crash.'

When Jesus had finished this discourse the people were as-

tounded at his teaching; unlike their own teachers he taught with
a note of authority.   —*Matthew 7:24–29*

HE TAUGHT IN PARABLES

On another occasion he began to teach by the lake-side. The
crowd that gathered round him was so large that he had to get into
a boat on the lake, and there he sat, with the whole crowd on the
beach right down to the water's edge. And he taught them many
things by parables.

As he taught he said:

'Listen! A sower went out to sow. And it happened that as he
sowed, some seed fell along the footpath; and the birds came and ate
it up. Some seed fell on rocky ground, where it had little soil, and it
sprouted quickly because it had no depth of earth; but when the
sun rose the young corn was scorched, and as it had no proper root
it withered away. Some seed fell among thistles; but the thistles
shot up and choked the corn, and it yielded no crop. And some
of the seed fell into good soil where it came up and grew, and bore
fruit; and the yield was thirtyfold, sixtyfold, even a hundredfold.'
He added, 'If you have ears to hear, then hear.'   —*Mark 4:1–9*

PARABLES ABOUT THE KINGDOM

He said, 'The kingdom of God is like this. A man scatters seed
on the land; he goes to bed at night and gets up in the morning, and
the seed sprouts and grows—how, he does not know. The ground
produces a crop by itself, first the blade, then the ear, then full-
grown corn in the ear; but as soon as the crop is ripe, he sets to work
with the sickle, because harvest-time has come.'

He said also, 'How shall we picture the kingdom of God, or by
what parable shall we describe it? It is like the mustard-seed, which
is smaller than any seed in the ground at its sowing. But once sown,
it springs up and grows taller than any other plant, and forms
branches so large that the birds can settle in its shade.'

—*Mark 4:26–32*

23

THE KINGDOM—AND JUDGMENT

Here is another parable that he put before them: 'The kingdom of Heaven is like this. A man sowed his field with good seed; but while everyone was asleep his enemy came, sowed darnel among the wheat, and made off. When the corn sprouted and began to fill out, the darnel could be seen among it. The farmer's men went to their master and said, "Sir, was it not good seed that you sowed in your field? Then where has the darnel come from?" "This is an enemy's doing", he replied. "Well then," they said, "shall we go and gather the darnel?" "No," he answered; "in gathering it you might pull up the wheat at the same time. Let them both grow together till harvest; and at harvest-time I will tell the reapers, 'Gather the darnel first, and tie it in bundles for burning; then collect the wheat into my barn.'"'   —*Matthew 13:24–30*

THE KINGDOM—AND COMMITMENT

'The kingdom of Heaven is like treasure lying buried in a field. The man who found it, buried it again; and for sheer joy went and sold everything he had, and bought that field.

'Here is another picture of the kingdom of Heaven. A merchant looking out for fine pearls found one of very special value; so he went and sold everything he had, and bought it.'

—*Matthew 13:44–46*

THE KINGDOM—AND FORGIVENESS

'The kingdom of Heaven, therefore, should be thought of in this way: There was once a king who decided to settle accounts with the men who served him. At the outset there appeared before him a man whose debt ran into millions. Since he had no means of paying, his master ordered him to be sold to meet the debt, with his wife, his children, and everything he had The man fell prostrate at his master's feet. "Be patient with me," he said, "and I will pay in full"; and the master was so moved with pity that he let the man go and remitted the debt. But no sooner had the man gone out than he met a fellow-servant who owed him a few pounds; and catching hold of him he gripped him by the throat and said, "Pay me what you owe." The man fell at his fellow-servant's feet, and begged him, "Be patient with me, and I will pay you"; but he refused, and had him jailed until he should pay the debt. The other servants were deeply distressed when they saw what had happened, and they went to their master and told him the whole story. He accordingly sent for the man. "You scoundrel!" he said to him; "I remitted the whole of your debt when you appealed to me; were you not bound to show your fellow-servant the same pity as I showed to you?" And so angry was the master that he condemned the man to torture until he should pay the debt in full. And that is how my heavenly Father will deal with you, unless you each forgive your brother from your hearts.'   —*Matthew 18:23–35*

THE KINGDOM—AND REWARDS

'The kingdom of Heaven is like this. There was once a landowner who went out early one morning to hire labourers for his vineyard; and after agreeing to pay them the usual day's wage he sent them off to work. Going out three hours later he saw some more men standing idle in the market-place. "Go and join the others in the vineyard," he said, "and I will pay you a fair wage"; so off they went. At noon he went out again, and at three in the afternoon, and made the same arrangement as before. An hour before sunset he went out and found another group standing there; so he said to them, "Why are you standing about like this all day with nothing to do?" "Because no one has hired us", they replied; so he told them, "Go and join the others in the vineyard." When evening fell, the owner of the vineyard said to his steward, "Call the labourers and give them their pay, beginning with those who came last and ending with the first." Those who had started work an hour before sunset came forward, and were paid the full day's wage. When it was the turn of the men who had come first, they expected something extra, but were paid the same amount as the others. As they took it, they grumbled at their employer: "These late-comers have done only one hour's work, yet you have put them on a level with us, who have sweated the whole day long in the blazing sun!" The owner turned to one of them and said, "My friend, I am not being unfair to you. You agreed on the usual wage for the day, did you not? Take your pay and go home. I choose to pay the last man the same as you. Surely I am free to do what I like with my own money. Why be jealous because I am kind?" Thus will the last be first, and the first last.'

—Matthew 20: 1–16

THE KINGDOM—
AND STEWARDSHIP OF TALENTS

'It [the kingdom of God] is like a man going abroad, who called his servants and put his capital in their hands; to one he gave five bags of gold, to another two, to another one, each according to his capacity. Then he left the country. The man who had the five bags went at once and employed them in business, and made a profit of five bags, and the man who had the two bags made two But the man who had been given one bag of gold went off and dug a hole in the ground, and hid his master's money. A long time afterwards their master returned, and proceeded to settle accounts with them. The man who had been given the five bags of gold came and produced the five he had made: "Master," he said "you left five bags with me; look, I have made five more." "Well done, my good and trusty servant!" said the master. "You have proved trustworthy in a small way; I will now put you in charge of something big. Come and share your master's delight." The man with the two bags then came and said, "Master, you left two bags with me; look, I have made two more." "Well done, my good and trusty servant!" said the master. "You have proved trustworthy in a small way; I will now put you in charge of something big. Come and share your master's delight." Then the man who had been given one bag came and said, "Master, I knew you to be a hard man: you reap where you have not sown, you gather where you have not scattered; so I was afraid, and I went and hid your gold in the ground. Here it is —you have what belongs to you." "You lazy rascal!" said the master. "You knew that I reap where I have not sown, and gather where I have not scattered? Then you ought to have put my money on deposit, and on my return I should have got it back with interest. Take the bag of gold from him, and give it to the one with the ten bags. For the man who has will always be given more, till he has enough and to spare; and the man who has not will forfeit even what he has. Fling the useless servant out into the dark, the place of wailing and grinding of teeth!" '   —*Matthew 25:14–30*

THE KINGDOM—LOVE AND JUDGMENT

'When the Son of Man comes in his glory and all the angels with him, he will sit in state on his throne, with all the nations gathered before him. He will separate men into two groups, as a shepherd separates the sheep from the goats, and he will place the sheep on his right hand and the goats on his left. Then the king will say to those on his right hand, "You have my Father's blessing; come, enter and possess the kingdom that has been ready for you since the world was made. For when I was hungry, you gave me food; when thirsty, you gave me drink; when I was a stranger you took me into your home, when naked you clothed me; when I was ill you came to my help, when in prison you visited me." Then the righteous will reply, "Lord, when was it that we saw you hungry and fed you, or thirsty and gave you drink, a stranger and took you home, or naked and clothed you? When did we see you ill or in prison, and come to visit you?" And the king will answer, "I tell you this: anything you did for one of my brothers here, however humble, you did for me." Then he will say to those on his left hand, "The curse is upon you; go from my sight to the eternal fire that is ready for the devil and his angels. For when I was hungry you gave me nothing to eat, when thirsty nothing to drink; when I was a stranger you gave me no home, when naked you did not clothe me; when I was ill and in prison you did not come to my help." And they too will reply, "Lord, when was it that we saw you hungry or thirsty or a stranger or naked or ill or in prison, and did nothing for you?" And he will answer, "I tell you this: anything you did not do for one of these, however humble, you did not do for me." And they will go away to eternal punishment, but the righteous will enter eternal life.'   —*Matthew 25:31–46*

PARABLES OF LOST THINGS

Another time, the tax-gatherers and other bad characters were all crowding in to listen to him; and the Pharisees and the doctors of the law began grumbling among themselves: 'This fellow', they said, 'welcomes sinners and eats with them.' He answered them with this parable: 'If one of you has a hundred sheep and loses one of them, does he not leave the ninety-nine in the open pasture and go after the missing one until he has found it? How delighted he is then! He lifts it on to his shoulders, and home he goes to call his friends and neighbours together. "Rejoice with me!" he cries. "I have found my lost sheep." In the same way, I tell you, there will be greater joy in heaven over one sinner who repents than over ninety-nine righteous people who do not need to repent.

'Or again, if a woman has ten silver pieces and loses one of them, does she not light the lamp, sweep out the house, and look in every corner till she has found it? And when she has, she calls her friends and neighbours together, and says, "Rejoice with me! I have found the piece that I lost." In the same way, I tell you, there is joy among the angels of God over one sinner who repents.'

Again he said: 'There was once a man who had two sons; and the younger said to his father, "Father, give me my share of the property." So he divided his estate between them. A few days later

28

the younger son turned the whole of his share into cash and left home for a distant country, where he squandered it in reckless living. He had spent it all, when a severe famine fell upon that country and he began to feel the pinch. So he went and attached himself to one of the local landowners, who sent him on to his farm to mind the pigs. He would have been glad to fill his belly with the pods that the pigs were eating; and no one gave him anything. Then he came to his senses and said, "How many of my father's paid servants have more food than they can eat, and here am I, starving to death! I will set off and go to my father, and say to him, 'Father, I have sinned, against God and against you; I am no longer fit to be called your son; treat me as one of your paid servants.'" So he set out for his father's house. But while he was still a long way off his father saw him, and his heart went out to him. He ran to meet him, flung his arms round him, and kissed him. The son said, "Father, I have sinned, against God and against you; I am no longer fit to be called your son." But the father said to his servants, "Quick! fetch a robe, my best one, and put it on him; put a ring on his finger and shoes on his feet. Bring the fatted calf and kill it, and let us have a feast to celebrate the day. For this son of mine was dead and has come back to life; he was lost and is found." And the festivities began.

'Now the elder son was out on the farm; and on his way back, as he approached the house, he heard music and dancing. He called one of the servants and asked what it meant. The servant told him, "Your brother has come home, and your father has killed the fatted calf because he has him back safe and sound." But he was angry and refused to go in. His father came out and pleaded with him; but he retorted, "You know how I have slaved for you all these years; I never once disobeyed your orders; and you never gave me so much as a kid, for a feast with my friends. But now that this son of yours turns up, after running through your money with his women, you kill the fatted calf for him." "My boy," said the father, "you are always with me, and everything I have is yours. How could we help celebrating this happy day? Your brother here was dead and has come back to life, was lost and is found." '

—Luke 15

A PARABLE ON PRIDE

And here is another parable that he told. It was aimed at those who were sure of their own goodness and looked down on everyone else. 'Two men went up to the temple to pray, one a Pharisee and the other a tax-gatherer. The Pharisee stood up and prayed thus: "I thank thee, O God, that I am not like the rest of men, greedy, dishonest, adulterous; or, for that matter, like this tax-gatherer. I fast twice a week; I pay tithes on all that I get." But the other kept his distance and would not even raise his eyes to heaven, but beat upon his breast, saying, "O God, have mercy on me, sinner that I am." It was this man, I tell you, and not the other, who went home acquitted of his sins. For everyone who exalts himself will be humbled; and whoever humbles himself will be exalted.'

—Luke 18:9–14

ABOUT RELIGIOUS TRADITIONS
AND INTEGRITY

A group of Pharisees, with some doctors of the law who had come from Jerusalem, met him and noticed that some of his disciples were eating their food with 'defiled' hands in other words, without washing them. (For the Pharisees and the Jews in general never eat without washing the hands, in obedience to an old-established tradition; and on coming from the market-place they never eat without first washing. And there are many other points on which they have a traditional rule to maintain, for example, washing of cups and jugs and copper bowls.) Accordingly, these Pharisees and the lawyers asked him, 'Why do your disciples not conform to the ancient tradition, but eat their food with defiled hands?' He answered, 'Isaiah was right when he prophesied about you hypocrites in these words: "This people pays me lip-service, but their heart is far from me: their worship of me is in vain, for they teach as doctrines the commandments of men." You neglect the commandment of God, in order to maintain the tradition of men.'

He also said to them, 'How well you set aside the commandment of God in order to maintain your tradition! Moses said, "Honour your father and your mother", and, "The man who curses his father or mother must suffer death." But you hold that if a man says to his father or mother, "Anything of mine which might have been used for your benefit is Corban"' (meaning, set apart for God), 'he is no longer permitted to do anything for his father or mother. Thus by your own tradition, handed down among you, you make God's word null and void. And many other things that you do are just like that.'

On another occasion he called the people and said to them, 'Listen to me, all of you, and understand this: nothing that goes into a man from outside can defile him; no, it is the things that come out of him that defile a man.'

When he had left the people and gone indoors, his disciples questioned him about the parable. He said to them, 'Are you as dull as the rest? Do you not see that nothing that goes from outside into a man can defile him, because it does not enter into his heart but into his stomach, and so passes out into the drain?' Thus he declared all foods clean. He went on, 'It is what comes out of a man that defiles him. For from inside, out of a man's heart, come evil thoughts, acts of fornication, of theft, murder, adultery, ruthless greed, and malice; fraud, indecency, envy, slander, arrogance, and folly; these evil things all come from inside, and they defile the man.'   —*Mark 7:1–23*

Even I began to see
What he was getting at;
He used such simple things,
Like coins and nets and pearls and seeds,
And light and birds and salt and yeast,
To help explain important thoughts
About integrity,
       and faith,
          the kingdom,
             and discipleship.

And I admire the way
He would attack hypocrisy,
Expose the selfish motives of men's hearts,
Unveil dishonesty,
And look with penetrating eyes at pride.

Yes, I begin to see
That what he said so long ago
Applies to me.

O holy Father, I am drawn to your Son. Drawn by the things he said, the way he lived. Sometimes his words are too deep for me to understand. Sometimes his teachings contradict much that the world teaches me.

It's hard to be meek in my kind of world.

It's hard to put others first, when you always have to compete.

It's hard to lose your life, when everyone says, "Be somebody."
Help me to live according to your will.
Forgive me when I fail. Amen.

IV MIRACLES: GOD'S POWER AND LOVE

The key word was: FAITH

As Jesus traveled about the countryside of Judea, he was deeply concerned about the suffering of the people. His heart went out to those who were hungry, to those possessed by evil spirits, to the lame and the deaf and the blind. But he was even more deeply concerned about the lame and deaf and blind human spirits.

When, in faith, they came to him to be healed, he said:
    "Your faith has cured you."
To the father of an epileptic boy he said:
    "Everything is possible to one who has faith."
To the disciples, frightened by the storm, he said:
    "Have you no faith?"

The key reason was: GOD'S POWER AND LOVE

Jesus was intent to make known the power and the love and the mercy of God. A power and love and mercy reaching out to each person, individually. When he cured Jairus' daughter, he gave the people strict orders not to tell what he had done. When he healed the mad man, he ordered them not to tell anyone that he had done it. Instead, he said:

    "Go home to your own folk and tell them what the Lord in his mercy has done for you."

And so, as Jesus ministered in Galilee and throughout Judea, the people were astonished, and praised God and said:

    "God has shown his care for his people."

STILLING THE STORM

That day, in the evening, he said to them, 'Let us cross over to the other side of the lake.' So they left the crowd and took him with them in the boat where he had been sitting; and there were other boats accompanying him. A heavy squall came on and the waves broke over the boat until it was all but swamped. Now he was in the stern asleep on a cushion; they roused him and said, 'Master, we are sinking! Do you not care?' He stood up, rebuked the wind, and said to the sea, 'Hush! Be still!' The wind dropped and there was a dead calm. He said to them, 'Why are you such cowards? Have you no faith even now?' They were awestruck and said to one another, 'Who can this be whom even the wind and the sea obey?'

—Mark 4:35–41

GOD'S HEALING POWER

So they came to the other side of the lake, into the country of the Gerasenes. As he stepped ashore, a man possessed by an unclean spirit came up to him from among the tombs where he had his dwelling. He could no longer be controlled; even chains were useless; he had often been fettered and chained up, but he had snapped his chains and broken the fetters. No one was strong enough to master him. And so, unceasingly, night and day, he would cry aloud among the tombs and on the hill-sides and cut himself with stones. When he saw Jesus in the distance, he ran and flung himself down before him, shouting loudly, 'What do you want with me, Jesus, son of the Most High God? In God's name do not torment me.' (For Jesus was already saying to him, 'Out, unclean spirit, come out of this man!') Jesus asked him, 'What is your name?' 'My name is Legion,' he said, 'there are so many of us.' And he begged hard that Jesus would not send them out of the country.

Now there happened to be a large herd of pigs feeding on the hill-side, and the spirits begged him, 'Send us among the pigs and let us go into them.' He gave them leave; and the unclean spirits came out and went into the pigs; and the herd, of about two thousand, rushed over the edge into the lake and were drowned.

The men in charge of them took to their heels and carried the news to the town and country-side; and the people came out to see what had happened. They came to Jesus and saw the madman who had been possessed by the legion of devils, sitting there clothed and in his right mind; and they were afraid. The spectators told them how the madman had been cured and what had happened to the pigs. Then they begged Jesus to leave the district.

As he was stepping into the boat, the man who had been possessed begged to go with him. Jesus would not allow it, but said to him, 'Go home to your own folk and tell them what the Lord in his mercy has done for you.' The men went off and spread the news in the Ten Towns of all that Jesus had done for him; and they were all amazed. —Mark 5:1–20

JAIRUS' DAUGHTER AND A SICK WOMAN

As soon as Jesus had returned by boat to the other shore, a great crowd once more gathered round him. While he was by the lakeside, the president of one of the synagogues came up, Jairus by name, and, when he saw him, threw himself down at his feet and pleaded with him. 'My little daughter', he said, 'is at death's door. I beg you to come and lay your hands on her to cure her and save her life.' So Jesus went with him, accompanied by a great crowd which pressed upon him.

Among them was a woman who had suffered from haemorrhages for twelve years; and in spite of long treatment by doctors, on which she had spent all she had, there had been no improvement; on the contrary, she had grown worse. She had heard what people were saying about Jesus, so she came up from behind in the crowd and touched his cloak; for she said to herself, 'If I touch even his clothes, I shall be cured.' And there and then the source of her haemorrhages dried up and she knew in herself that she was cured of her trouble. At the same time Jesus, aware that power had gone out of him, turned round in the crowd and asked, 'Who touched my clothes?' His disciples said to him, 'You see the crowd pressing upon you and yet you ask, "Who touched me?"' Meanwhile he was looking round to see who had done it. And the woman, trembling with fear when she grasped what had happened to her, came and fell at his feet and told him the whole truth. He said to her, 'My daughter, your faith has cured you. Go in peace, free for ever from this trouble.'

While he was still speaking, a message came from the president's house, 'Your daughter is dead; why trouble the Rabbi further?' But Jesus, overhearing the message as it was delivered, said to the president of the synagogue, 'Do not be afraid; only have faith.' After this he allowed no one to accompany him except Peter and James and James's brother John. They came to the president's house, where he found a great commotion, with loud crying and wailing. So he went in and said to them, 'Why this crying and commotion? The child is not dead: she is asleep.' But they only laughed at him. After turning all the others out, he took the child's father and mother and his own companions and went in where the child was lying. Then, taking hold of her hand, he said to her, 'Talitha cum', which means, 'Get up, my child.' Immediately the girl got up and walked about—she was twelve years old. At that they were beside themselves with amazement. He gave them strict orders to let no one hear about it, and told them to give her something to eat.

—Mark 5: 21–43

FEEDING THE MULTITUDE

He [Jesus] said to them, 'Come with me, by yourselves, to some lonely place where you can rest quietly.' (For they had no leisure even to eat, so many were coming and going.) Accordingly, they set off privately by boat for a lonely place. But many saw them leave and recognized them, and came round by land, hurrying from all the towns towards the place, and arrived there first. When he came ashore, he saw a great crowd; and his heart went out to them, because they were like sheep without a shepherd; and he had much to teach them. As the day wore on, his disciples approached him and said, 'This is a lonely place and it is getting very late; send the people off to the farms and villages round about, to buy themselves something to eat.' 'Give them something to eat yourselves', he answered. They replied, 'Are we to go and spend twenty pounds on bread to give them a meal?' 'How many loaves have you?' he asked; 'go and see.' They found out and told him, 'Five, and two fishes also.' He ordered them to make the people sit down in groups on the green grass, and they sat down in rows, a hundred rows of fifty each. Then, taking the five loaves and the two fishes, he looked up to heaven, said the blessing, broke the loaves, and gave them to the disciples to distribute. He also divided the two fishes among them. They all ate to their hearts' content; and twelve great basketfuls of scraps were picked up, with what was left of the fish. Those who ate the loaves numbered five thousand men.   —Mark 6: 31–44

HEALING A DEAF MAN

On his return journey from Tyrian territory he went by way of Sidon to the Sea of Galilee through the territory of the Ten Towns. They brought to him a man who was deaf and had an impediment in his speech, with the request that he would lay his hand on him. He took the man aside, away from the crowd, put his fingers into his ears, spat, and touched his tongue. Then, looking up to heaven, he sighed, and said to him, 'Ephphatha', which means 'Be opened.' With that his ears were opened, and at the same time the impediment was removed and he spoke plainly. Jesus forbade them to tell anyone; but the more he forbade them, the more they published it. Their astonishment knew no bounds: 'All that he does, he does well,' they said; 'he even makes the deaf hear and the dumb speak.'   —Mark 7: 31–37

THE WIDOW'S SON

Afterwards Jesus went to a town called Nain, accompanied by his disciples and a large crowd. As he approached the gate of the town he met a funeral. The dead man was the only son of his widowed mother; and many of the townspeople were there with her. When the Lord saw her his heart went out to her, and he said, 'Weep no more.' With that he stepped forward and laid his hand on the bier; and the bearers halted. Then he spoke: 'Young man, rise up!' The dead man sat up and began to talk; and Jesus gave him back to his mother. Deep awe fell upon them all, and they praised God. 'A great prophet has arisen among us', they said, and again, 'God has shown his care for his people.' The story of what he had done ran through all parts of Judea and the whole neighbourhood.

—Luke 7:11–17

HEALING AN EPILEPTIC

When they came back to the disciples they saw a large crowd surrounding them and lawyers arguing with them. As soon as they saw Jesus the whole crowd were overcome with awe, and they ran forward to welcome him. He asked them, 'What is this argument about?' A man in the crowd spoke up: 'Master, I brought my son to you. He is possessed by a spirit which makes him speechless. Whenever it attacks him, it dashes him to the ground, and he foams at the mouth, grinds his teeth, and goes rigid. I asked your disciples to cast it out, but they failed.' Jesus answered: 'What an unbelieving and perverse generation! How long shall I be with you? How long must I endure you? Bring him to me.' So they brought the boy to him; and as soon as the spirit saw him it threw the boy into convulsions, and he fell on the ground and rolled about foaming at the mouth. Jesus asked his father, 'How long has he been like this?' 'From childhood,' he replied; 'often it has tried to make an end of him by throwing him into the fire or into water. But if it is at all possible for you, take pity upon us and help us.' 'If it is possible!' said Jesus. 'Everything is possible to one who has faith.' 'I have faith,' cried the boy's father; 'help me where faith falls short.' Jesus saw then that the crowd was closing in upon them, so he rebuked the unclean spirit. 'Deaf and dumb spirit,' he said, 'I command you, come out of him and never go back!' After crying aloud and racking him fiercely, it came out; and the boy looked like a corpse; in fact, many said, 'He is dead.' But Jesus took his hand and raised him to his feet, and he stood up.

Then Jesus went indoors, and his disciples asked him privately, 'Why could not we cast it out?' He said, 'There is no means of casting out this sort but prayer.'   —*Mark 9: 14–29*

I'm not so sure about those miracles,
I don't see things like that happening today.
What really went on, anyway?
Did they just make up all those things?
But then, why should they lie?
I just don't understand . . .

He looked with great compassion on the hungry crowd,
They seemed like sheep needing to be fed.
And there was fish and bread
Enough for all.

                    Did it really happen?

The angry seas and winds
Were hushed and still.

                    I can't believe it!

A little girl was dead—
"Get up, my child."

                    It's really amazing!

The blind, the deaf, the lame
Stumbled to his side,
And they were healed.

                    Astonishing!

Creator God, when I consider the moon and stars, the universe and
galaxies, I am amazed at your greatness and your power. What is man
that you even bother with him? Do you really know and care about each
and every individual person? How can you? My mind is too small to
imagine all this.

If you do love and care for everyone, why did you allow miracles
in some places, and let other people suffer and get killed? I guess my
mind is too small to understand this also.

Help me, Amen.

V FOLLOW ME

Hans Memling   CHRIST AS SAVIOR OF THE WORLD

John asked the question outright—the question that had been growing in people's minds ever since Jesus began to teach and heal.

"Are you the one who is to come?"
And Jesus replied, "Tell John what you have seen, and heard
  —the blind recover their sight,
  —the lame walk,
  —the lepers are clean,
  —the deaf hear,
  —the dead are raised to life,
  —the poor are hearing the good news."
John had to decide for himself.

Then, alone with his disciples, Jesus knew that the time had come. He knew that the scribes and Pharisees were plotting against him. He realized that there would be trouble ahead—persecution, even death. He knew his little band of followers would need to be strong. They needed to affirm for themselves that he was indeed the Son of God.

And so he asked:
  "Who do you say I am?"
And Peter replied:
  "You are the Messiah."
There, it had been said at last!
  "You are the Messiah, the Son of the living God!"

And later, while they worshiped on a mountaintop, it was as if God himself confirmed their affirmation with the words:
  "This is my Son, . . . listen to him."
There was no doubt about it now!

But what did it mean? What did it mean for them?
  A kingdom? Special honor? Special privileges?
NO! It meant a new kind of kingdom. Being part of it meant serving humbly. It meant self-denial, risk, and suffering. It meant a cross.

But it also meant—eternal life!

ARE YOU THE ONE?

John too was informed of all this by his disciples. Summoning two of their number he sent them to the Lord with this message: 'Are you the one who is to come, or are we to expect some other?' The messengers made their way to Jesus and said, 'John the Baptist has sent us to you: he asks, "Are you the one who is to come, or are we to expect some other?" ' There and then he cured many sufferers from diseases, plagues, and evil spirits; and on many blind people he bestowed sight. Then he gave them his answer: 'Go', he said, 'and tell John what you have seen and heard: how the blind recover their sight, the lame walk, the lepers are clean, the deaf hear, the dead are raised to life, the poor are hearing the good news—and happy is the man who does not find me a stumbling-block.'

After John's messengers had left, Jesus began to speak about him to the crowds: 'What was the spectacle that drew you to the wilderness? A reed-bed swept by the wind? No? Then what did you go out to see? A man dressed in silks and satins? Surely you must look in palaces for grand clothes and luxury. But what did you go out to see? A prophet? Yes indeed, and far more than a prophet. He is the man of whom Scripture says,

"Here is my herald, whom I send on ahead of you,
    And he will prepare your way before you."

I tell you, there is not a mother's son greater than John, and yet the least in the kingdom of God is greater than he.'

When they heard him, all the people, including the tax-gatherers, praised God, for they had accepted John's baptism; but the Pharisees and lawyers, who refused his baptism, had rejected God's purpose for themselves.

'How can I describe the people of this generation? What are they like? They are like children sitting in the market-place and shouting at each other,

"We piped for you and you would not dance."

"We wept and wailed, and you would not mourn."

For John the Baptist came neither eating bread nor drinking wine, and you say, "He is possessed." The Son of Man came eating and drinking, and you say, "Look at him! a glutton and a drinker, a friend of tax-gatherers and sinners!" And yet God's wisdom is proved right by all who are her children.'   —*Luke 7:18–35*

WHO DO YOU SAY I AM?

Jesus and his disciples set out for the villages of Caesarea Philippi. On the way he asked his disciples, 'Who do men say I am?' They answered, 'Some say John the Baptist, others Elijah, others one of the prophets.' 'And you,' he asked, 'who do you say I am?' Peter replied: 'You are the Messiah.' Then he gave them strict orders not to tell anyone about him; and he began to teach them that the Son of Man had to undergo great sufferings, and to be rejected by the elders, chief priests, and doctors of the law; to be put to death, and to rise again three days afterwards. He spoke about it plainly. At this Peter took him by the arm and began to rebuke him. But Jesus turned round, and, looking at his disciples, rebuked Peter. 'Away with you, Satan,' he said; 'you think as men think, not as God thinks.'

Then he called the people to him, as well as his disciples, and said to them, 'Anyone who wishes to be a follower of mine must leave self behind; he must take up his cross, and come with me. Whoever cares for his own safety is lost; but if a man will let himself be lost for my sake and for the Gospel, that man is safe. What does a man gain by winning the whole world at the cost of his true self? What can he give to buy that self back? If anyone is ashamed of me and mine in this wicked and godless age, the Son of Man will be ashamed of him, when he comes in the glory of his Father and of the holy angels.'   —*Mark 8:27–38*

THIS IS MY SON

Six days later Jesus took Peter, James, and John with him and led them up a high mountain where they were alone; and in their presence he was transfigured; his clothes became dazzling white, with a whiteness no bleacher on earth could equal. They saw Elijah appear, and Moses with him, and there they were, conversing with Jesus. Then Peter spoke: 'Rabbi,' he said, 'how good it is that we are here! Shall we make three shelters, one for you, one for Moses, and one for Elijah?' (For he did not know what to say; they were so terrified.) Then a cloud appeared, casting its shadow over them, and out of the cloud came a voice: 'This is my Son, my Beloved; listen to him.' And now suddenly, when they looked around, there was nobody to be seen but Jesus alone with themselves.

On their way down the mountain, he enjoined them not to tell anyone what they had seen until the Son of Man had risen from the dead. They seized upon those words, and discussed among themselves what this 'rising from the dead' could mean. And they put a question to him: 'Why do our teachers say that Elijah must be the first to come?' He replied, 'Yes, Elijah does come first to set everything right. Yet how is it that the scriptures say of the Son of Man that he is to endure great sufferings and to be treated with contempt? However, I tell you, Elijah has already come and they have worked their will upon him, as the scriptures say of him.'

—*Mark 9: 2–13*

BE LIKE CHILDREN

So they came to Capernaum; and when he was indoors, he asked them, 'What were you arguing about on the way?' They were silent, because on the way they had been discussing who was the greatest. He sat down, called the Twelve, and said to them, 'If anyone wants to be first, he must make himself last of all and servant of all.' Then he took a child, set him in front of them, and put his arm round him. 'Whoever receives one of these children in my name', he said, 'receives me; and whoever receives me, receives not me but the One who sent me.'

—*Mark 9: 33–37*

They brought children for him to touch; and the disciples scolded them for it. But when Jesus saw this he was indignant, and said to them, 'Let the children come to me; do not try to stop them; for the kingdom of God belongs to such as these. I tell you, whoever does not accept the kingdom of God like a child will never enter it.' And he put his arms round them, laid his hands upon them, and blessed them. —*Mark 10:13–16*

SEEK ETERNAL LIFE

As he was starting out on a journey, a stranger ran up, and, kneeling before him, asked, 'Good Master, what must I do to win eternal life?' Jesus said to him, 'Why do you call me good? No one is good except God alone. You know the commandments: "Do not murder; do not commit adultery; do not steal; do not give false evidence; do not defraud; honour your father and mother." ' 'But, Master,' he replied, 'I have kept all these since I was a boy.' Jesus looked straight at him; his heart warmed to him, and he said, 'One thing you lack: go, sell everything you have, and give to the poor, and you will have riches in heaven; and come, follow me.' At these words his face fell and he went away with a heavy heart; for he was a man of great wealth.

Jesus looked round at his disciples and said to them, 'How hard it will be for the wealthy to enter the kingdom of God!' They were amazed that he should say this, but Jesus insisted, 'Children, how hard it is to enter the kingdom of God! It is easier for a camel to pass through the eye of a needle than for a rich man to enter the kingdom of God.' They were more astonished than ever, and said to one another, 'Then who can be saved?' Jesus looked them in the face and said, 'For men it is impossible, but not for God; to God everything is possible.'

At this Peter spoke. 'We here', he said, 'have left everything to become your followers.' Jesus said, 'I tell you this: there is no one who has given up home, brothers or sisters, mother, father or children, or land, for my sake and for the Gospel, who will not receive in this age a hundred times as much—houses, brothers and sisters, mothers and children, and land—and persecutions besides; and in the age to come eternal life. But many who are first will be last and the last first.'

—Mark 10: 17–31

SERVE HUMBLY

They were on the road, going up to Jerusalem, Jesus leading the way; and the disciples were filled with awe; while those who followed behind were afraid. He took the Twelve aside and began to tell them what was to happen to him. 'We are now going to Jerusalem,' he said; 'and the Son of Man will be given up to the chief priests and the doctors of the law; they will condemn him to death and hand him over to the foreign power. He will be mocked and spat upon, flogged and killed; and three days afterwards, he will rise again.'

James and John, the sons of Zebedee, approached him and said, 'Master, we should like you to do us a favour.' 'What is it you want me to do?' he asked. They answered, 'Grant us the right to sit in state with you, one at your right and the other at your left.' Jesus said to them, 'You do not understand what you are asking. Can you drink the cup that I drink, or be baptized with the baptism I am baptized with?' 'We can', they answered. Jesus said, 'The cup that I drink you shall drink, and the baptism I am baptized with shall be your baptism; but to sit at my right or left is not for me to grant; it is for those to whom it has already been assigned.'

When the other ten heard this, they were indignant with James and John. Jesus called them to him and said, 'You know that in the world the recognized rulers lord it over their subjects, and their great men make them feel the weight of authority. That is not the way with you; among you, whoever wants to be great must be your servant, and whoever wants to be first must be the willing slave of all. For even the Son of Man did not come to be served but to serve, and to surrender his life as a ransom for many.' —Mark 10: 32–45

50

WHO AM I REALLY?

Who am I?
I have asked myself a hundred times.
Who am I, really?
Where am I going? What am I to be?
A whole lifetime lies ahead of me.

Then, suddenly—
    your question comes:
        "Who do you say *I* am?"

And I resent this bold intrusion on my thoughts.
    Who are *you?*
        What is that to me?
The important thing to me—is *me!*

You ask again,
More than a question—a command:
    "Who do you say I am?"

And there is silence for an hour or so,
While in the restless corridors of me
Some words take shape,
And then resound
With all the sharpness of a bright, new day—
    "You are the Christ,
        The Son of the Living God!
        My Lord. My King."

And there is silence for an hour or so,
While I am wondering
    —about God's purpose for his people here on earth,
    —about all those in ages past who witnessed and who served,
    —about God's will for me.

Then, I hear echoing:
    "Take up your cross, and follow me!"

Father God, I thank you for your son, Jesus Christ. For his life of
discipline and service, I am grateful. For his reverence and love, I now
give thanks. I am glad that those who knew him wrote down the things
he said and did. Help me also to follow him. Amen.

VI CHALLENGE AT JERUSALEM

15th Century Rhenish Master　　　CHRIST ON HORSEBACK

He was so strong, so sure.
They saw it in his face, steadfastly set.
He moved with confidence—
    toward Jerusalem.
He knew what lay ahead, and yet
He lived each moment to the full—

"Hosanna in the heavens."
    "Blessings on him who comes in the name of the Lord!"
Ride on, O King!

He moved with confidence within the temple courts,
Meeting the tricky inquiries
Of Pharisees and Sadducees,
On their own ground,
With stature and with poise.

His mind, so filled with faith, and love
Found equal place for logic,
    reasoning,
        and clever thought,
Yet, did not overlook the widow's coin.

He was so strong, so sure, so confident,
And yet so sad, those last days in Jerusalem.

ENTERING JERUSALEM

They were now approaching Jerusalem, and when they reached Bethphage and Bethany, at the Mount of Olives, he sent two of his disciples with these instructions: 'Go to the village opposite, and, just as you enter, you will find tethered there a colt which no one has yet ridden. Untie it and bring it here. If anyone asks, "Why are you doing that?", say, "Our Master needs it, and will send it back here without delay." ' So they went off, and found the colt tethered to a door outside in the street. They were untying it when some of the bystanders asked, 'What are you doing, untying that colt?' They answered as Jesus had told them, and were then allowed to take it. So they brought the colt to Jesus and spread their cloaks on it, and he mounted. And people carpeted the road with their cloaks, while others spread brushwood which they had cut in the fields; and those who went ahead and the others who came behind shouted, 'Hosanna! Blessings on him who comes in the name of the Lord! Blessings on the coming kingdom of our father David! Hosanna in the heavens!'   —*Mark 11:1–10*

UPSETTING THE TEMPLE

So they came to Jerusalem, and he went into the temple and began driving out those who bought and sold in the temple. He upset the tables of the money-changers and the seats of the dealers in pigeons; and he would not allow anyone to use the temple court as a thoroughfare for carrying goods. Then he began to teach them, and said, 'Does not Scripture say, "My house shall be called a house of prayer for all the nations"? But you have made it a robbers' cave.' The chief priests and the doctors of the law heard of this and sought some means of making away with him; for they were afraid of him, because the whole crowd was spellbound by his teaching. And when evening came he went out of the city.   —*Mark 11:15–19*

55

CHALLENGE OF AUTHORITY

They came once more to Jerusalem. And as he was walking in the temple court the chief priests, lawyers, and elders came to him and said, 'By what authority are you acting like this? Who gave you authority to act in this way?' Jesus said to them, 'I will ask you one question; and if you give me an answer, I will tell you by what authority I act. The baptism of John: was it from God, or from men? Answer me.' This set them arguing among themselves: 'What shall we say? If we say, "from God", he will say, "Then why did you not believe him?" Shall we say, "from men"?'—but they were afraid of the people, for all held that John was in fact a prophet. So they answered Jesus, 'We do not know.' And Jesus said to them, 'Then neither will I tell you by what authority I act.'

He went on to speak to them in parables: 'A man planted a vineyard and put a wall round it, hewed out a winepress, and built a watch-tower; then he let it out to vine-growers and went abroad. When the vintage season came, he sent a servant to the tenants to collect from them his share of the produce. But they took him, thrashed him, and sent him away empty-handed. Again, he sent them another servant, whom they beat about the head and treated outrageously. So he sent another, and that one they killed; and many more besides, of whom they beat some, and killed others. He had now only one left to send, his own dear son. In the end he sent him. "They will respect my son", he said. But the tenants said to one another, "This is the heir; come, let us kill him, and the property will be ours." So they seized him and killed him, and flung his body out of the vineyard. What will the owner of the vineyard do? He will come and put the tenants to death and give the vineyard to others.

'Can it be that you have never read this text: "The stone which the builders rejected has become the main corner-stone. This is the Lord's doing, and it is wonderful in our eyes"?'

Then they began to look for a way to arrest him, for they saw that the parable was aimed at them; but they were afraid of popular feeling, so they left him alone and went away.

—*Mark 11:27—12:12*

TRICK QUESTIONS

A number of Pharisees and men of Herod's party were sent to trap him with a question. They came and said, 'Master, you are an honest man, we know, and truckle to no man, whoever he may be; you teach in all honesty the way of life that God requires. Are we or are we not permitted to pay taxes to the Roman Emperor? Shall we pay or not?' He saw how crafty their question was, and said, 'Why are you trying to catch me out? Fetch me a silver piece, and let me look at it.' They brought one, and he said to them, 'Whose head is this, and whose inscription?' 'Caesar's', they replied. Then Jesus said, 'Pay Caesar what is due to Caesar, and pay God what is due to God.' And they heard him with astonishment.

Next Sadducees came to him. (It is they who say that there is no resurrection.) Their question was this: 'Master, Moses laid it down for us that if there are brothers, and one dies leaving a wife but no child, then the next should marry the widow and carry on his brother's family. Now there were seven brothers. The first took a wife and died without issue. Then the second married her, and he too died without issue. So did the third. Eventually the seven of them died, all without issue. Finally the woman died. At the resurrection, when they come back to life, whose wife will she be, since all seven had married her?' Jesus said to them, 'You are mistaken, and surely this is the reason: you do not know either the scriptures or the power of God. When they rise from the dead, men and women do not marry; they are like angels in heaven.

'Now about the resurrection of the dead, have you never read in the Book of Moses, in the story of the burning bush, how God

57

spoke to him and said, "I am the God of Abraham, the God of Isaac, and the God of Jacob"? God is not God of the dead but of the living. You are greatly mistaken.' —*Mark 12:13–27*

AN HONEST INQUIRY

Then one of the lawyers, who had been listening to these discussions and had noted how well he answered, came forward and asked him, 'Which commandment is first of all?' Jesus answered, 'The first is, "Hear, O Israel: the Lord your God is the only Lord; love the Lord your God with all your heart, with all your soul, with all your mind, and with all your strength." The second is this: "Love your neighbour as yourself." There is no other commandment greater than these.' The lawyer said to him, 'Well said, Master. You are right in saying that God is one and beside him there is no other. And to love him with all your heart, all your understanding, and all your strength, and to love your neighbour as yourself—that is far more than any burnt offerings or sacrifices.' When Jesus saw how sensibly he answered, he said to him, 'You are not far from the kingdom of God.'

After that nobody ventured to put any more questions to him.
  —*Mark 12:28–34*

HYPOCRISY AND GENUINENESS

There was a great crowd and they listened eagerly. He said as he taught them, 'Beware of the doctors of the law, who love to walk up and down in long robes, receiving respectful greetings in the street; and to have the chief seats in synagogues, and places of honour at feasts. These are the men who eat up the property of widows, while they say long prayers for appearance' sake, and they will receive the severest sentence.'

Once he was standing opposite the temple treasury, watching as people dropped their money into the chest. Many rich people were giving large sums. Presently there came a poor widow who dropped in two tiny coins, together worth a farthing. He called his disciples to him. 'I tell you this,' he said: 'this widow has given more than

any of the others; for those others who have given had more than enough, but she, with less than enough, has given all that she had to live on.'
                                                              —*Mark 12:37b–44*

WORDS OF WARNING

As he was leaving the temple, one of his disciples exclaimed, 'Look, Master, what huge stones! What fine buildings!' Jesus said to him, 'You see these great buildings? Not one stone will be left upon another; all will be thrown down.'

When he was sitting on the Mount of Olives facing the temple he was questioned privately by Peter, James, John, and Andrew: 'Tell us,' they said, 'when will this happen? What will be the sign when the fulfilment of all this is at hand?'

Jesus began: 'Take care that no one misleads you. Many will come claiming my name, and saying, "I am he"; and many will be misled by them.

'When you hear the noise of battle near at hand and the news of battles far away, do not be alarmed. Such things are bound to happen; but the end is still to come. For nation will make war upon nation, kingdom upon kingdom; there will be earthquakes in many places; there will be famines. With these things the birth-pangs of the new age begin.

'As for you, be on your guard. You will be handed over to the courts. You will be flogged in synagogues. You will be summoned to appear before governors and kings on my account to testify in their presence. But before the end the Gospel must be proclaimed to all nations. So when you are arrested and taken away, do not worry beforehand about what you will say, but when the time comes say whatever is given you to say; for it will not be you that speak, but the Holy Spirit. Brother will betray brother to death, and the father his child; children will turn against their parents and send them to their death. All will hate you for your allegiance to me; but the man who holds out to the end will be saved.'
                                                              —*Mark 13:1–13*

59

At first I wondered if he was just trying to be heroic or something.
Why go to Jerusalem when you know there is going to be trouble?
Why ask for it?
Why not go back to Galilee?
He must have had some other things to teach,
And there were lots of people left to heal.
He could have done a lot of good.
    I wonder how he was so sure
    That he was right
    About Jerusalem.

And then I got to wondering
How I would feel if I knew
I had but one week to live.

What would I do?
    Maybe write a book
    About everything that was important to me.
        But he never wrote a word.
        How could he trust his followers
        To remember things, and tell them right?
    Or maybe, if I had one week to live,
    I'd be especially nice to everyone,
    So they would remember me
    As being kind and good.
        But he got angry with the money-changers,
        Said, "Beware of the doctors of the law."
        He met their tricky questions
        With such honesty.

I wonder how he stayed so poised and confident.
That last week.

Father God, how can I be wise enough to stop, and think, and pray
when I am young and eager to get on with things? Guide me through
the tricky questions of my day: popularity, the gang, new clothes,
prejudices. Help me to live courageously, regardless of the conse-
quences. Help me to know when the time is right to take a stand—in
school, with friends, on the athletic field, at home. Grant me confidence
born of trust in thee. Amen.

VII FINAL CONFLICT

It Was a Holiday in Palestine . . .

For hundreds of years the Jewish people had remembered God's great deeds to them, his people. Especially they remembered how God had delivered them from bondage in Egypt to freedom in a new land. Families gathered for a special memorial feast, the Passover meal,
> a time for celebration,
> a time for worship.

It Was a Holy Day in an Upper Room . . .

Jesus and his disciples met together for a special meal, their last meal together. Quietly they shared in the last supper, and he talked with them
> about his death,
> about a deeper fellowship,
> about love for one another,
> about the kingdom of God.

And then he went out to the Garden of Gethsemane to pray.

It Was a Horrible Day in Jerusalem . . .

Judas betrayed him. Jesus was seized and brought to trial. Peter denied him. His disciples fled. Jesus was questioned and scoffed,
> beaten and mocked,
> crucified,
> and buried.

Bernard Buffet   THE THREE CROSSES

PREPARATIONS FOR DEATH

Now the Festival of Passover and Unleavened Bread was only two days off; and the chief priests and the doctors of the law were trying to devise some cunning plan to seize him and put him to death. 'It must not be during the festival,' they said, 'or we should have rioting among the people.'

Jesus was at Bethany, in the house of Simon the leper. As he sat at table, a woman came in carrying a small bottle of very costly perfume, oil of pure nard. She broke it open and poured the oil over his head. Some of those present said to one another angrily, 'Why this waste? The perfume might have been sold for thirty pounds and the money given to the poor'; and they turned upon her with fury. But Jesus said, 'Let her alone. Why must you make trouble for her? It is a fine thing she has done for me. You have the poor among you always, and you can help them whenever you like; but you will not always have me. She has done what lay in her power; she is beforehand with anointing my body for burial. I tell you this: wherever in all the world the Gospel is proclaimed, what she has done will be told as her memorial.'

Then Judas Iscariot, one of the Twelve, went to the chief priests to betray him to them. When they heard what he had come for, they were greatly pleased, and promised him money; and he began to look for a good opportunity to betray him.   —*Mark 14:1–11*

THE LAST SUPPER

Now on the first day of Unleavened Bread, when the Passover lambs were being slaughtered, his disciples said to him, 'Where would you like us to go and prepare for your Passover supper?' So he sent out two of his disciples with these instructions: 'Go into the city, and a man will meet you carrying a jar of water. Follow him, and when he enters a house give this message to the householder: "The Master says, 'Where is the room reserved for me to eat the Passover with my disciples?'" He will show you a large room upstairs, set out in readiness. Make the preparations for us there.' Then the disciples went off, and when they came into the city they found everything just as he had told them. So they prepared for Passover.

In the evening he came to the house with the Twelve. As they sat at supper Jesus said, 'I tell you this: one of you will betray me— one who is eating with me.' At this they were dismayed; and one by one they said to him, 'Not I, surely?' 'It is one of the Twelve', he said, 'who is dipping into the same bowl with me. The Son of Man is going the way appointed for him in the scriptures; but alas for that man by whom the Son of Man is betrayed! It would be better for that man if he had never been born.'

During supper he took bread, and having said the blessing he broke it and gave it to them, with the words: 'Take this; this is my body.' Then he took a cup, and having offered thanks to God he gave it to them; and they all drank from it. And he said, 'This is my blood of the covenant, shed for many. I tell you this: never again shall I drink from the fruit of the vine until that day when I drink it new in the kingdom of God.' —*Mark 14:12–25*

FAREWELL WORDS

'If you dwell in me, and my words dwell in you, ask what you will, and you shall have it. This is my Father's glory, that you may bear fruit in plenty and so be my disciples. As the Father has loved me, so I have loved you. Dwell in my love. If you heed my commands, you will dwell in my love, as I have heeded my Father's commands and dwell in his love.

'I have spoken thus to you, so that my joy may be in you, and your joy complete. This is my commandment: love one another, as I have loved you. There is no greater love than this, that a man should lay down his life for his friends. You are my friends, if you do what I command you. I call you servants no longer; a servant does not know what his master is about. I have called you friends, because I have disclosed to you everything that I heard from my Father. You did not choose me: I chose you. I appointed you to go on and bear fruit, fruit that shall last; so that the Father may give you all that you ask in my name. This is my commandment to you: love one another.'

—John 15:7–17

A PRAYER

After these words Jesus looked up to heaven and said:

'Father, the hour has come. Glorify thy Son, that the Son may glorify thee. For thou hast made him sovereign over all mankind, to give eternal life to all whom thou hast given him. This is eternal life: to know thee who alone art truly God, and Jesus Christ whom thou hast sent.

*   *   *   *

'And now I am coming to thee; but while I am still in the world I speak these words, so that they may have my joy within them in full measure. I have delivered thy word to them, and the world hates them because they are strangers in the world, as I am. I pray thee, not to take them out of the world, but to keep them from the evil one. They are strangers in the world, as I am. Consecrate them by the truth; thy word is truth. As thou hast sent me into the world, I have sent them into the world, and for their sake I now consecrate myself, that they too may be consecrated by the truth.'

—John 17:1–3, 13–19

IN GETHSEMANE

After singing the Passover Hymn, they went out to the Mount of Olives. And Jesus said, 'You will all fall from your faith; for it stands written: "I will strike the shepherd down and the sheep will be scattered." Nevertheless, after I am raised again I will go on before you into Galilee.' Peter answered, 'Everyone else may fall away, but I will not.' Jesus said, 'I tell you this: today, this very night, before the cock crows twice, you yourself will disown me three times.' But he insisted and repeated: 'Even if I must die with you, I will never disown you.' And they all said the same.

66

When they reached a place called Gethsemane, he said to his disciples, 'Sit here while I pray.' And he took Peter and James and John with him. Horror and dismay came over him, and he said to them, 'My heart is ready to break with grief; stop here, and stay awake.' Then he went forward a little, threw himself on the ground, and prayed that, if it were possible, this hour might pass him by. 'Abba, Father,' he said, 'all things are posible to thee; take this cup away from me. Yet not what I will, but what thou wilt.'

He came back and found them asleep; and he said to Peter, 'Asleep, Simon? Were you not able to keep awake for one hour? Stay awake, all of you; and pray that you may be spared the test: the spirit is willing, but the flesh is weak.' Once more he went away and prayed. On his return he found them asleep again, for their eyes were heavy; and they did not know how to answer him.

The third time he came and said to them, 'Still sleeping? Still taking your ease? Enough! The hour has come. The Son of Man is betrayed to sinful men. Up, let us go forward! My betrayer is upon us.'

Suddenly, while he was still speaking, Judas, one of the Twelve, appeared, and with him was a crowd armed with swords and cudgels, sent by the chief priests, lawyers, and elders. Now the traitor had agreed with them upon a signal: 'The one I kiss is your man; seize him and get him safely away.' When he reached the spot, he stepped forward at once and said to Jesus, 'Rabbi', and kissed him. Then they seized him and held him fast.

One of the party drew his sword, and struck at the High Priest's servant, cutting off his ear. Then Jesus spoke: 'Do you take me for a bandit, that you have come out with swords and cudgels to arrest me? Day after day I was within your reach as I taught in the temple, and you did not lay hands on me. But let the scriptures be fulfilled.' Then the disciples all deserted him and ran away.

Among those following was a young man with nothing on but a linen cloth. They tried to seize him; but he slipped out of the linen cloth and ran away naked. · —*Mark 14 : 26–52*

TRIAL BEFORE THE HIGH PRIEST

Then they led Jesus away to the High Priest's house, where the chief priests, elders, and doctors of the law were all assembling. Peter followed him at a distance right into the High Priest's courtyard; and there he remained, sitting among the attendants, warming himself at the fire.

The chief priests and the whole Council tried to find some evidence against Jesus to warrant a death-sentence, but failed to find any. Many gave false evidence against him, but their statements did not tally. Some stood up and gave this false evidence against him: 'We heard him say, "I will throw down this temple, made with human hands, and in three days I will build another, not made with hands." ' But even on this point their evidence did not agree.

Then the High Priest stood up in his place and questioned Jesus: 'Have you no answer to the charges that these witnesses bring against you?' But he kept silence; he made no reply.

Again the High Priest questioned him: 'Are you the Messiah, the Son of the Blessed One?' Jesus said, 'I am; and you will see the Son of Man seated on the right hand of God and coming with the clouds of heaven.' Then the High Priest tore his robes and said, 'Need we call further witnesses? You have heard the blasphemy. What is your opinion?' Their judgement was unanimous: that he was guilty and should be put to death.

Some began to spit on him, blindfolded him, and struck him with their fists, crying out, 'Prophesy!' And the High Priest's men set upon him with blows.

Meanwhile Peter was still in the courtyard downstairs. One of the High Priest's serving-maids came by and saw him there warming himself. She looked into his face and said, 'You were there too, with this man from Nazareth, this Jesus.' But he denied it: 'I know nothing,' he said; 'I do not understand what you mean.' Then he went outside into the porch; and the maid saw him there again and began to say to the bystanders, 'He is one of them'; and again he denied it.

Again, a little later, the bystanders said to Peter, 'Surely you are one of them. You must be; you are a Galilean.' At this he broke out into curses, and with an oath he said, 'I do not know this man you speak of.' Then the cock crew a second time; and Peter remembered how Jesus had said to him, 'Before the cock crows twice you will disown me three times.' And he burst into tears.   —*Mark 14:53–72*

TRIAL BEFORE PILATE

When morning came the chief priests, having made their plan with the elders and lawyers and all the Council, put Jesus in chains; then they led him away and handed him over to Pilate. Pilate asked him, 'Are you the king of the Jews?' He replied, 'The words are yours.' And the chief priests brought many charges against him. Pilate questioned him again: 'Have you nothing to say in your defence? You see how many charges they are bringing against you.' But, to Pilate's astonishment, Jesus made no further reply.

At the festival season the Governor used to release one prisoner at the people's request. As it happened, the man known as Barabbas was then in custody with the rebels who had committed murder in the rising. When the crowd appeared asking for the usual favour, Pilate replied, 'Do you wish me to release for you the king of the Jews?' For he knew it was out of spite that they had brought Jesus before him. But the chief priests incited the crowd to ask him to release Barabbas rather than Jesus. Pilate spoke to them again: 'Then what shall I do with the man you call king of the Jews?' They shouted back, 'Crucify him!' 'Why, what harm has he done?' Pilate asked. They shouted all the louder, 'Crucify him!' So Pilate, in his desire to satisfy the mob, released Barabbas to them; and he had Jesus flogged and handed him over to be crucified.

Then the soldiers took him inside the courtyard (the Governor's headquarters) and called together the whole company. They dressed him in purple, and having plaited a crown of thorns, placed it on his head. Then they began to salute him with, 'Hail, King of the Jews!' They beat him about the head with a cane and spat upon him, and then knelt and paid mock homage to him. When they had finished their mockerey, they stripped him of the purple and dressed him in his own clothes.   —*Mark 15:1–20*

THE CRUCIFIXION

Then they took him out to crucify him. A man called Simon, from Cyrene, the father of Alexander and Rufus, was passing by on his way in from the country, and they pressed him into service to carry his cross.

They brought him to the place called Golgotha, which means 'Place of a skull'. He was offered drugged wine, but he would not take it. Then they fastened him to the cross. They divided his clothes among them, casting lots to decide what each should have.

The hour of the crucifixion was nine in the morning, and the inscription giving the charge against him read, 'The king of the Jews.' Two bandits were crucified with him, one on his right and the other on his left.

The passers-by hurled abuse at him: 'Aha!' they cried, wagging their heads, 'you would pull the temple down, would you, and build it in three days? Come down from the cross and save your-self!' So too the chief priests and the doctors of the law jested with one another: 'He saved others,' they said, 'but he cannot save him-self. Let the Messiah, the king of Israel, come down now from the cross. If we see that, we shall believe.' Even those who were cru-cified with him taunted him.

At midday darkness fell over the whole land, which lasted till three in the afternoon; and at three Jesus cried aloud, *'Eli, Eli, lema sabachthani?'*, which means, 'My God, my God, why hast thou forsaken me?' Some of the passers-by, on hearing this, said, 'Hark, he is calling Elijah.' A man came running with a sponge, soaked in sour wine, on the end of a cane, and held it to his lips. 'Let us see', he said, 'if Elijah is coming to take him down.' Then Jesus gave a loud cry and died. And the curtain of the temple was torn in two from top to bottom. And when the centurion who was standing opposite him saw how he died, he said, 'Truly this man was a son of God.' —*Mark 15:20b–39*

A number of women were also present, watching from a distance. Among them were Mary of Magdala, Mary the mother of James the younger and of Joseph, and Salome, who had all followed him and waited on him when he was in Galilee, and there were several others who had come up to Jerusalem with him.

By this time evening had come; and as it was Preparation-day (that is, the day before the Sabbath), Joseph of Arimathaea, a respected member of the Council, a man who was eagerly awaiting the kingdom of God, bravely went in to Pilate and asked for the body of Jesus. Pilate was surprised to hear that he was already dead; so he sent for the centurion and asked him whether it was long since he died. And when he heard the centurion's report, he gave Joseph leave to take the dead body. So Joseph bought a linen sheet, took him down from the cross, and wrapped him in the sheet. Then he laid him in a tomb cut out of the rock, and rolled a stone against the entrance. And Mary of Magdala and Mary the mother of Joseph were watching and saw where he was laid. —*Mark 15:40–47*

Can it be that all this happened in one day?

The upper room,
    the bread and wine,
        Gethsemane,
            the trials, mockery,
                the cross.
The waiting,
    and the dying,
        and the grave.

It almost seems as if all time,
    and all eternity,
Converged in this one place
    for this one awful day.

As if the judgment of all time,
    and the suffering of all space,
Had met on this one hill,
    at this one cross.

I cannot hope to understand fully
All that took place on that one day,
That Thursday night through Friday night,
And yet I sense a difference
    in all of time,
Because of that one day.

O God, forgive me.

THE UPPER ROOM
By claiming to be part of your fellowship,
And then selling out to other interests,
I betray you, daily.

GETHSEMANE
By neglecting to worship,
By forgetting to pray,
I am unfaithful.

THE COURTYARD
By evading the truth,
By pretending not to understand,
By refusing to admit that I know him,
I deny my Lord.

PILATE'S HOUSE
By being so anxious to please the crowd,
By letting others take the responsibility or blame,
I mock him.

CALVARY
By my own sin and selfishness,
By closing out the cries of human need and anguish,
I crucify.

O God, forgive me. Forgive me. Amen.

VIII THE VICTORY

Piero della Francesca   **RESURRECTION**

It was all over, finished,
  THE END.

The disciples of Jesus were discouraged and bewildered,
They couldn't understand it at all.
  Their hopes were smashed.
  They had believed him;
  They had followed him.
He had promised a kingdom.
  And now he was crucified, dead.

And then it happened.
The women came rushing back from the tomb—terrified.
The tomb was empty! Incredible!

Slowly, surely, it dawned on them—
  HE WAS ALIVE!

Jesus walked with them along a road.
He came and stood in their midst.
He talked with them by the lakeside.
Astonishing!
  THE LORD HAD RISEN!

As he spoke to them they felt new power surging in their hearts.
  "Peace be with you."
  "Receive the Holy Spirit."
They sensed new life, new purpose, a call to mission.
  "Feed my sheep."
  "Go—make all nations my disciples."

And so, what they thought was *the end* . . .
  was really only *the beginning!*

THE EMPTY TOMB

When the Sabbath was over, Mary of Magdala, Mary the mother of James, and Salome bought aromatic oils intending to go and anoint him; and very early on the Sunday morning, just after sunrise, they came to the tomb. They were wondering among themselves who would roll away the stone for them from the entrance to the tomb, when they looked up and saw that the stone, huge as it was, had been rolled back already. They went into the tomb, where they saw a youth sitting on the right-hand side, wearing a white robe; and they were dumbfounded. But he said to them, 'Fear nothing; you are looking for Jesus of Nazareth, who was crucified. He has risen; he is not here; look, there is the place where they laid him. But go and give this message to his disciples and Peter: "He will go on before you into Galilee and you will see him there, as he told you." ' Then they went out and ran away from the tomb, beside themselves with terror. They said nothing to anybody, for they were afraid.   —*Mark 16: 1–8*

THE RISEN LORD

That same day two of them were on their way to a village called Emmaus, which lay about seven miles from Jerusalem, and they were talking together about all these happenings. As they talked and discussed it with one another, Jesus himself came up and walked along with them; but something held their eyes from seeing who it was. He asked them, 'What is it you are debating as you walk?' They halted, their faces full of gloom, and one, called Cleopas, answered, 'Are you the only person staying in Jerusalem not to know what has happened there in the last few days?' 'What do you mean?' he said. 'All this about Jesus of Nazareth,' they replied, 'a prophet powerful in speech and action before God and the whole people; how our chief priests and rulers handed him over to be sentenced to death, and crucified him. But we had been hoping that he was the man to liberate Israel. What is more, this is the third day since it happened, and now some women of our company have astounded us: they went early to the tomb, but failed to find his body, and returned with a story that they had seen a vision of angels who told them he was alive. So some of our people went to the tomb and found things just as the women had said; but him they did not see.'

'How dull you are!' he answered. 'How slow to believe all that the prophets said! Was the Messiah not bound to suffer thus before entering upon his glory?' Then he began with Moses and all the prophets, and explained to them the passages which referred to himself in every part of the scriptures.

By this time they had reached the village to which they were going, and he made as if to continue his journey, but they pressed him: 'Stay with us, for evening draws on, and the day is almost over.' So he went in to stay with them. And when he had sat down with them at table, he took bread and said the blessing; he broke the bread, and offered it to them. Then their eyes were opened, and they recognized him; and he vanished from their sight. They said to one another, 'Did we not feel our hearts on fire as he talked with us on the road and explained the scriptures to us?'

Without a moment's delay they set out and returned to Jerusalem. There they found that the Eleven and the rest of the company had assembled, and were saying, 'It is true: the Lord has risen; he has appeared to Simon.' Then they gave their account of the events of their journey and told how he had been recognized by them at the breaking of the bread.   —*Luke 24:13–35*

THE HOLY SPIRIT

Late that Sunday evening, when the disciples were together behind locked doors, for fear of the Jews, Jesus came and stood among them. 'Peace be with you!' he said, and then showed them his hands and his side. So when the disciples saw the Lord, they were filled with joy. Jesus repeated, 'Peace be with you!', and then said, 'As the Father sent me, so I send you.' He then breathed on them, saying, 'Receive the Holy Spirit!' —*John 20: 19–22*

LOVE AND SERVE GOD

Some time later, Jesus showed himself to his disciples once again, by the Sea of Tiberias; and in this way. Simon Peter and Thomas 'the Twin' were together with Nathanael of Cana-in-Galilee. The sons of Zebedee and two other disciples were also there. Simon Peter said, 'I am going out fishing.' 'We will go with you', said the others. So they started and got into the boat. But that night they caught nothing.

Morning came, and there stood Jesus on the beach, but the disciples did not know that it was Jesus. He called out to them, 'Friends, have you caught anything?' They answered 'No.' He said, 'Shoot the net to starboard, and you will make a catch.' They did so, and found they could not haul the net aboard, there were so many fish in it. Then the disciple whom Jesus loved said to Peter, 'It is the Lord!' When Simon Peter heard that, he wrapped his coat about him (for he had stripped) and plunged into the sea. The rest of them came on in the boat, towing the net full of fish; for they were not far from land, only about a hundred yards.

When they came ashore, they saw a charcoal fire there, with fish laid on it, and some bread. Jesus said, 'Bring some of your catch.' Simon Peter went aboard and dragged the net to land, full of big fish, a hundred and fifty-three of them; and yet, many as they were, the net was not torn. Jesus said, 'Come and have breakfast.' None of the disciples dared to ask 'Who are you?' They knew it was the Lord. Jesus now came up, took the bread, and gave it to them, and the fish in the same way.

*   *   *   *

After breakfast, Jesus said to Simon Peter, 'Simon son of John, do you love me more than all else?' 'Yes, Lord,' he answered, 'you know that I love you.' 'Then feed my lambs', he said. A second time he asked, 'Simon son of John, do you love me?' 'Yes, Lord, you know I love you.' 'Then tend my sheep.' A third time he said, 'Simon son of John, do you love me?' Peter was hurt that he asked him a third time, 'Do you love me?' 'Lord,' he said, 'you know everything; you know I love you.' Jesus said, 'Feed my sheep.'

—John 21:1–13, 15–17

BE MY WITNESSES

The eleven disciples made their way to Galilee, to the mountain where Jesus had told them to meet him. When they saw him, they fell prostrate before him, though some were doubtful. Jesus then came up and spoke to them. He said: 'Full authority in heaven and on earth has been committed to me. Go forth therefore and make all nations my disciples; baptize men everywhere in the name of the Father and the Son and the Holy Spirit, and teach them to observe all that I have commanded you. And be assured, I am with you always, to the end of time.'   *—Matthew 28:16–20*

THE POWER AND THE GLORY-FOREVER

While the day of Pentecost was running its course they were all together in one place, when suddenly there came from the sky a noise like that of a strong driving wind, which filled the whole house where they were sitting. And there appeared to them tongues like flames of fire, dispersed among them and resting on each one. And they were all filled with the Holy Spirit and began to talk in other tongues, as the Spirit gave them power of utterance.

Now there were living in Jerusalem devout Jews drawn from every nation under heaven; and at this sound the crowd gathered, all bewildered because each one heard the apostles talking in his own language. They were amazed and in their astonishment exclaimed, 'Why, they are all Galileans, are they not, these men who are speaking? How is it then that we hear them, each of us in his own native language?' . . . And they were all amazed and perplexed, saying to one another, 'What can this mean?' Others said contemptuously, 'They have been drinking!'

But Peter stood up with the Eleven, raised his voice, and addressed them: 'Fellow Jews, and all you who live in Jerusalem, mark this and give me a hearing. These men are not drunk, as you imagine; for it is only nine in the morning. No, this is what the prophet spoke of: "God says, 'This will happen in the last days: I will pour out upon everyone a portion of my spirit; and your sons and daughters shall prophesy; your young men shall see visions, and your old men shall dream dreams. Yes, I will endue even my slaves, both men and women, with a portion of my spirit, and they shall prophesy. . . .' "

'Men of Israel, listen to me: I speak of Jesus of Nazareth, a man singled out by God and made known to you through miracles, portents, and signs, which God worked among you through him, as you well know. When he had been given up to you, by the deliberate will and plan of God, you used heathen men to crucify and kill him. But God raised him to life again, setting him free from the pangs of death, because it could not be that death should keep him in its grip.'

* * * *

When they heard this they were cut to the heart, and said to Peter and the apostles, 'Friends, what are we to do?' 'Repent,' said Peter, 'repent and be baptized, every one of you, in the name of Jesus the Messiah for the forgiveness of your sins; and you will receive the gift of the Holy Spirit. For the promise is to you, and to your children, and to all who are far away, everyone whom the Lord our God may call.'

In these and many other words he pressed his case and pleaded with them: 'Save yourselves', he said, 'from this crooked age.' Then those who accepted his word were baptized, and some three thousand were added to their number that day.

They met constantly to hear the apostles teach, and to share the common life, to break bread, and to pray. A sense of awe was everywhere, and many marvels and signs were brought about through

the apostles. All whose faith had drawn them together held everything in common: they would sell their property and possessions
and make a general distribution as the need of each required. With
one mind they kept up their daily attendance at the temple, and,
breaking bread in private houses, shared their meals with unaf-
fected joy, as they praised God and enjoyed the favour of the whole
people. And day by day the Lord added to their number those
whom he was saving.   —*Acts 2:1–8, 12–18, 22–24, 37–47*

My heart sings:

THINE IS THE KINGDOM . . .

"The sovereignty of the world has passed to our Lord
and his Christ, and he shall reign for ever and ever!"

AND THE POWER . . .

"He is risen!"
"God raised him to life again—because it could not be that
death should keep him in its grip!"

AND THE GLORY . . .

"Receive the Holy Spirit."
"And they were all filled with the Holy Spirit!"
"The promise is to you, and to your children,
    and to all who are far away."
"To him be glory in the church!"

FOR EVER . . .

"Go forth therefore and make all nations my disciples;
baptize men everywhere in the name of the Father, and the
Son, and the Holy Spirit, and teach them to observe all
that I have commanded you. And be assured, I am with you
always, to the end of time."

AMEN

"There were indeed many other signs that Jesus performed in the
presence of his disciples, which are not recorded in this book. Those
here written have been recorded in order that you may hold the faith
that Jesus is the Christ, the Son of God, and that through this faith
you may possess eternal life by his name."   —*John 20:30–31*

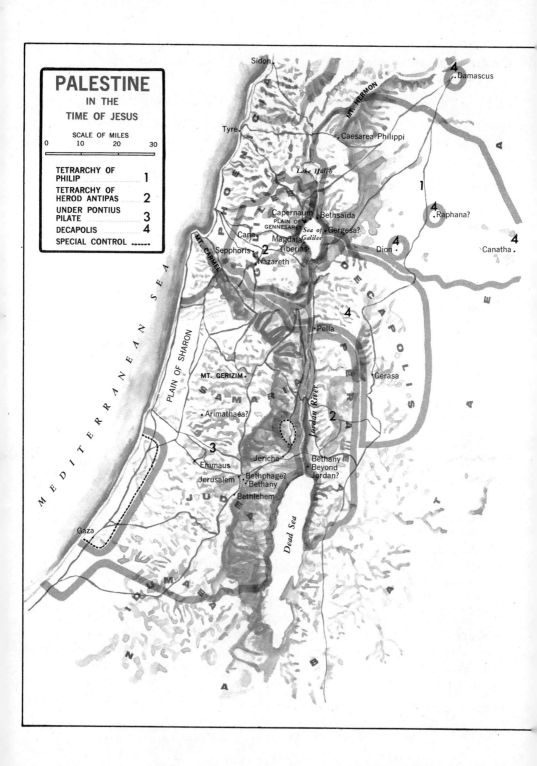

PALESTINE
IN THE
TIME OF JESUS

SCALE OF MILES
0   10   20   30

TETRARCHY OF PHILIP 1
TETRARCHY OF HEROD ANTIPAS 2
UNDER PONTIUS PILATE 3
DECAPOLIS 4
SPECIAL CONTROL ------

Sidon

Damascus

Tyre

Caesarea Philippi

MT. HERMON

Lake Huleh

Raphana?

Capernaum   Bethsaida
PLAIN OF
GENNESARET   Sea of   Gergesa?
Cana   Galilee
Magdala   Tiberias   Dion
Sepphoris 2   Canatha
Nazareth

MT. CARMEL

DECAPOLIS

MEDITERRANEAN SEA

PLAIN OF SHARON

Pella

MT. GERIZIM

SAMARIA

Gerasa

Arimathaea?

Jordan River

2

3

Emmaus   Jericho   Bethany
Jerusalem   Bethphage?   Beyond
            Bethany   Jordan?
            Bethlehem

JUDAEA

Gaza

Dead Sea

IDUMAEA

Glossary and Pronunciation Guide

ABIATHAR (ə-bī'-ə-thər)—priest in the time of David.

ALPHAEUS (ăl-fē'-ŭs)—father of Levi (Matthew).

ARIMATHAEA (ăr-ə-mə-thē-'ə)—home of the rich member of the Jewish Council in whose tomb Jesus was buried.

BARABBAS (bər-ăb'-əs)—the prisoner released by Pilate at the trial of Jesus in response to the demands of the crowd.

BETHANY (bĕth'-a-nĭ)—town near Jerusalem, home of Mary and Martha.

BETHPHAGE (bĕth'-fə-jĭ)—village near Jerusalem from which Jesus began his triumphal entry.

BETHSAIDA (bĕth-sā'-ə-də)—town on the north shore of the Sea of Galilee; home of Peter, Andrew, and Philip.

BOANERGES (bō-ə-nûr'-jēz)—name meaning "sons of thunder" given by Jesus to James and John.

CAESAREA PHILIPPI (sĕs-ə-rē'-ə fĭ-lĭp'-ī)—gentile city near Mount Hermon near which Peter made his confession.

CANA (kā'-nə)—village in Galilee, near Nazareth.

CAPURNAUM (kä-pûr'-na-ŭm)—city on the northwest shore of the Sea of Galilee, center of much of Jesus' work.

CLEOPAS (klē'-ə-păs)—one of the two disciples who met the risen Jesus on the Emmaus road.

CORBAN (kôr'-băn)—an offering set aside for God and therefore not to be used for other purposes.

CYRENE (sī-rē'-nĭ)—principal city of Libya in North Africa.

DARNEL (därn'l)—a kind of grass; a weed in a field of wheat.

ELIJAH (ĕ-lī'-jə)—prophet of the ninth century B.C.

EMMAUS (ĕ-mā'-ŭs)—village six to seven miles from Jerusalem, site of one of Jesus' resurrection appearances.

GERASENES (gĕr'-ə-sēnz, also Gergesenes)—inhabitants of Gerasa, probably located on the eastern shore of the Sea of Galilee; site of Jesus' healing of the man with the devils.

GETHSEMANE (gĕth-sĕm'-ə-nĭ)—a garden on the Mount of Olives outside Jerusalem where Jesus was arrested.

GOLGOTHA (gŏl'-gə-thə)—place outside the wall of Jerusalem where Jesus was crucified.

GOSPEL—the good news of God's love made known in Jesus Christ.

IDUMAEA (ĭd-o͞o-mē'-ə)—region in southern Palestine.

ISAIAH (ī-zā'-ə)—great prophet of the eighth century B.C.

JAIRUS (jā'-ĭ-rŭs)—president of a synagogue in Galilee whose daughter was cured by Jesus.

ā able; ă mat; ä calm; ē equal; ĕ set; ī ice; ĭ sit; ō over; ŏ box; ô saw; o͞o ooze; ū use; ŭ up; û urge; ə for a alone; e system; i easily; o gallop; u circus.

Magdala (măg′-də-lə)—town on the western shore of the Sea of Galilee.

Nain (nā′-ĭn)—a small village six miles southeast of Nazareth.

nard—a fragrant ointment made from spikenard which grows in the Himalaya Mountains.

Pentecost (pĕn′-tĭ-kôst)—Jewish agricultural festival occurring fifty days after the Passover.

Pharisees (făr′-ə-sēz)—members of one of the religious groups in Judaism in the time of Jesus, made up of middle-class layman utterly devoted to keeping the Jewish religious law.

Pilate, Pontius (pī′-lət, pŏn′-shus)—Roman governor of Judaea, Samaria, and Idumaea (A.D. 26–36).

Sadducees (săd′-ə-sēz)—members of one of the religious groups in Judaism in the time of Jesus, made up of conservative, upper-class people who favored cooperation with the Romans.

Salome (sə-lō′-mĭ)—one of the women who witnessed Jesus' crucifixion and went to the tomb to anoint his body.

Samaria (sə-mār′-ĭ-ə)—region in central Palestine south of Galilee.

Sidon (sī′-dŏn)—ancient Phoenician city on the Mediterranean Sea located in present day Lebanon.

Ten Towns—ten Greek cities mostly located across the Jordan River from the region of Galilee.

Thaddaeus (thăd′-ē-əs)—one of the twelve disciples.

Tiberias, Sea of (tī-bēr′-ĭ-us)—another name for the Sea of Galilee.

Tyre (tīr)—seaport in modern Lebanon important throughout biblical history.

Zealot (zĕl′-ŭt)—member of a group of Jewish patriots opposed to Roman rule.

Index

HEALINGS

INCIDENTS

PARABLES

TEACHINGS